W9-BJR-598

AMY FRYKHOLM

a contemplative biography

JULIAN

of Norwich

PARACLETE PRESS
BREWSTER, MASSACHUSETTS

Julian of Norwich: A Contemplative Biography
2018 Second Paperback Printing
2011 First Paperback Printing
2010 First Hardcover Printing

ISBN 978-1-61261-097-9

The Paraclete Press name and logo (dove and cross) are trademarks of Paraclete Press, Inc.

The Library of Congress has catalogued the hardcover edition as follows:
Frykholm, Amy Johnson, 1971-
  Julian of Norwich : a contemplative biography / Amy Frykholm.
     p. cm.
  Includes bibliographical references (p.   ).
  ISBN 978-1-55725-626-3
  1. Julian, of Norwich, b. 1343. 2. Women mystics—England—Biography.
I. Title.
  BV5095.J84F79 2010
  282.092—dc22
  [B]   2010009417

10 9 8 7 6 5 4 3 2

Published by Paraclete Press
Brewster, Massachusetts
www.paracletepress.com
Printed in the United States of America

This book is dedicated to my mother,
MICHELE JOHNSON,
who has faithfully modeled
attention to the
lowly and simple things.

Contents

Introduction

IN THE MIDST OF WHAT HISTORIAN BARBARA TUCHMAN has called the "calamitous" fourteenth century—marked by war, famine, plague, and unrest—one woman wrote a book. It was the first book composed by a woman in English and remains one of the greatest theological works in the English language. So little is known about this woman that even her name—Julian of Norwich—is in question. Yet her achievement is extraordinary. Very few people—male or female—at that time wrote anything in English. As the language of the common people, English was rarely used for literary purposes. But Julian's achievement isn't just in having written a book in English, but in the nature of what she had to say.

Playfully and subtly maneuvering amid political dangers and social limitations, with open curiosity and dry humor, Julian took a heavy world of religious obligation and turned it on its head. In her book, which is both an account of visions she received and a book of spiritual direction and theological reflection, she wrote, "The soul must perform two duties. One is that we reverently marvel. The other is that we humbly endure, ever taking pleasure in God." In Julian's understanding, the right relationship between God and the soul was not primarily guilt for sin, but wonder, release, and unity. She wrote that the righteousness required of us was simply this: delight in God's good world.

This delight travels a hard road through Julian's writing, as it did through her life. To reach delight, Julian had to traverse the suffering she saw all around her and experienced herself, and then actively choose compassion. Eventually, she saw that God and the soul shared something so intimate that even sin could not disrupt it—the soul and God were one.

Perhaps even more strikingly, Julian saw herself, a laywoman, as representative of all Christians, and she believed that the visions she had received were meant for all. Her writing, of necessity, took on a prophetic tone as she tried to peer forward to a time when God would use her writing for his own "honorable, marvelous, and plenteous" work.

At last in our own day, Julian's writings have reached a wide audience. Dozens of current translations, devotional books, and anthologies suggest that Julian's words reach the present with striking urgency. We are hungry to understand this God whose love encloses us. We ache to understand that the soul is intricately "oned" both to the body and to God. We desire to act in the world as full creatures, wholly loved. Julian becomes, almost inexplicably, a teacher for our times. Yet we experience discomfort in confronting Julian's suffering Christ. For contemporary readers, Julian's declaration that at a young age she "desired . . . a bodily sickness" coupled with her gory depictions of Christ bleeding on the cross are off-putting and impenetrable. This contradiction has made Julian both a welcome voice and a distant one. To overcome that distance, we must gain a better understanding of her life.

THE REVOLUTIONARY ACT OF REENVISIONING the relationship between God and the soul and then writing it down was done quietly, in solitude, on the far eastern coast of England in the river port city of Norwich. In her book, Julian writes that at the age of thirty, she became seriously ill—so ill that she and all of those around her thought she would die. In the midst of this mysterious illness, Christ appeared to her as in the passion of his crucifixion. And over the course of several hours, Christ revealed to her the mystery of his compassion.

During her visions and for decades afterward, Julian wrestled with understanding what she had seen. The God of her visions and the God of the church to which she was devoted contradicted each other, sometimes painfully. The church in Julian's time was beginning to take violent measures to protect its power. By the time Julian took up a pen putting words to parchment, the church hierarchy had actively banned the use of English in religious contexts, except in sermons, confessions, and other practical matters. People were carried out of the city gates of Norwich and burnt if an English-language Bible was discovered in their homes.

In this context of fear, the crucified Jesus taught Julian that she was utterly safe in his love. Safety did not come from bowing to the forces of fear. Instead, it came from submitting oneself in love to the one who is love. As if reflecting on her precarious position—as a woman writing a religious book in English—Julian wrote that love itself kept her safe. "And thus will I love, and thus do I love, and thus I am safe."

A sense of spiritual safety alone was not enough for a woman in the Middle Ages to undertake the writing of a book. She needed to seek solitude and relief from everyday burdens. One of the few things we know for certain about Julian is that in the middle of her life she went to live in an anchorage—a small solitary cell—next to St. Julian's church in Norwich, dedicating herself to prayer and dwelling next to the church until the end of her life. Perhaps she took her name from this church; perhaps the similarity is mere coincidence.

The majority of anchorites (coming from the Greek, meaning "to withdraw") in Julian's time were, like Julian, women from the Norfolk region of England. Traditionally, an anchorage was a small cell—sometimes just one room—with three windows. These windows were the sole openings for the anchoress onto the world. One window opened to the church, where an anchoress could hear the daily mass. Another window opened onto a servant's quarters, through which daily life transpired. A third window opened onto a small porch, through which the anchoress received visitors.

It was common practice for the people of the parish to support an anchoress with food, clothing, and shelter. They believed that her prayers, in turn, supported them. Indeed, the main duty of the anchoress was to pray for the people of the parish, both the living and the dead. Anchoresses also fulfilled another function. Through the small porch window, the anchoress acted as counselor, hearing people's stories and offering advice.

It was in this context and for these people that Julian wrote her book, so that the guidance offered at the window would be ongoing in another form beyond her cell. Breathtaking for its daring, Julian's book was formed outside the structures of the church hierarchy, not for clerics or even for nuns, but for her "even Christians," the common people of the church whom she loved. At extraordinary personal risk and with extraordinary dedication, she wrote what reads, in ways, like a private and intimate letter to friends, but with such theological depth and stunning insight that six hundred years later we continue to be instructed and transformed.

Her language use, as it developed, was a mix of the spiritual and the material. Her images—hazelnuts, herring, pellets, eaves—were drawn from everyday life and were meant to remind her readers that we are united with God even through our physical being. Julian's language had the quality of finely made homespun. Crafted, yes, but refined, no. It had echoes of stories told around peat fires and the smell of their smoke, of rhymes and songs sung by mothers to their children.

This work, shaped by decades of prayer and meditation, was offered to the world through the small window of a solitary's cell. Somehow, even miraculously, it survives to delight and hearten us today.

IN JULIAN'S CASE, GAINING A BETTER UNDERSTANDING of her life is particularly difficult. As with most women in the Middle Ages, we have very little documentary evidence to work from. At the same time, all biography is an act of empathetic imagination. We read and write it to try to walk alongside someone who is far away from us in time and space. To walk alongside Julian, imagination plays a crucial role. Poet Denise Levertov has called Julian's life a "medieval enigma." We have little in the way of historical records to guide us. We do not know for certain if Julian married, if she became a nun, or if she had children. We do not know which social class she came from or how she received the education that allowed her to write her book. The centuries that separate us are a chasm.

Just as if we were approaching the anchorage window, what we see of Julian will be limited and even obscured. The "windows" through which we might see her hide as much as they reveal. And yet, every detail helps us to understand and imagine the world from which she came. Julian herself gives us permission, in a sense, for this inquiry, as she tells us that in the smallest detail—a hazelnut—the vastness of the world and its love by God can be known. In the hints that her text and the historical record give us, Julian steps forward.

In biography, we look for Julian first through her own texts. In what follows, I have chosen specific moments from her writing that are particularly revelatory of her life. I have called such moments "windows"—and fortunately, we have more than three through which we can look. Julian writes, of course, as a self-conscious artist, choosing carefully what details to give us. Hours and hours of meditation shape every word she offers of her own experience. She does not intend for this manuscript to be about herself, but instead to point toward the God of love who revealed himself to her.

Her book, *A Revelation of Love,* was written in two versions. The earlier version is often simply called *The Short Text* because it lacks a title. In the only existing copy, included in a medieval compendium of devotional writings, a scribe begins, abruptly, with these words, "There is an anchoress—be the goodness of God," and then Julian's own arresting and personal voice tells the story of her visionary experience.

The second version of Julian's book is dramatically longer and theologically richer and more daring. God appears in this book as a mother, and Jesus' death on the cross is interpreted as childbearing labor. Julian also describes Jesus as both a gardener and an impoverished itinerant laborer. To produce this text, Julian writes that she spent twenty years meditating on her visions. In that time, a great deal of insight was granted to her. Between the two versions, Julian sheds fear and anxiety, both about her visions and about the act of writing. She writes with stunning freedom and peace. While there are excerpts from this book in another medieval manuscript, we have no medieval example of it in its entirety. Instead, we have three copies in all probability taken from the same original scribed by a group of Benedictine nuns living in France in the seventeenth century.

This means that the version of Julian's words that has come to us has passed through many hands before reaching ours. Her manuscript was hand copied and recopied perhaps dozens or hundreds of times. We cannot be certain that what we have is exactly the text created by Julian herself. Furthermore, unfortunately, we have nothing written in Julian's own hand.

Yet when we read *A Revelation of Love*, we hear Julian speaking to us directly, without intermediaries. Her voice is unique, personal, and intimate. The chasm of six hundred years suddenly closes, and we have no doubt that the woman speaking to us lived and breathed, and that her voice was as meaningful in her own day as it is in ours. The immediacy and relevance of her words startle and amaze. The uniqueness and power of her voice awaken and stir us.

IN ADDITION TO JULIAN'S OWN TEXTS, we have a slim historical record that confirms at least the outlines of Julian's life. Medieval people believed that the prayers of the living helped to propel the dead from purgatory to paradise. Those who could left money in the form of bequests to remind the living to pray for them after their deaths. Anchorites, in particular, received this money because their prayers were considered especially effectual. In addition, anchorites offered much-needed solace and advice for the living, and gifts of gratitude were offered for spiritual direction and teaching.

Julian received four such bequests, an unusually small number for a woman who lived many years in the anchorage and who has had such an extended and profound influence. Of course, only the wealthy could leave a record of their gifts, and likely dozens of other grateful, but poorer, parishioners left more perishable records of their appreciation. What the four bequests left for "Dame Julian" tell us is that she was enclosed in the anchorage by 1393, around the age of fifty. This is the date when she received her first bequest. She died sometime after 1416—the date of the last bequest. While the number of bequests is small, their variety is remarkable: a countess, a lawyer, a chantry priest, and a rector. In other words, though she lived enclosed as a solitary and we have no record of anyone reading her book in her lifetime, her life touched people far beyond her cell.

We have one other outside confirmation of Julian's life from her own day. Not far from Norwich, a woman named Margery Kempe wrote, via scribes, an autobiographical manuscript. Thirty years younger than Julian, Margery was the daughter of a government official and the wife of a merchant. A restless spiritual seeker, she embarked on pilgrimages all over the medieval world and consulted endlessly with spiritual guides and counselors.

Early in her book, Margery described traveling to Norwich to visit some of the great spiritual lights of that city. At Julian's cell, she conversed with the now-aged anchoress. Once again, Julian's resonant voice arises unmistakably through the pages. Margery's account allows us to envision Julian as counselor and guide, a woman who greeted her guests with generosity of spirit and no small amount of truth.

While this historical record offers little, medieval historian Carole Hill notes that women's history nearly always has to be told this way: through the cracks and fissures. In any given medieval document, women's activities and lives are concealed. If we are going to tell their stories, we must make choices based on sometimes paltry evidence. Two things are crucial: that we proceed with humility and that we do not imagine the people of the Middle Ages to be less human than we are.

I have occasionally made controversial choices. Since the first widely distributed modern version of Julian's writings in 1901, most people have assumed that Julian was an extraordinarily well-educated aristocratic woman. Many believe that she was a Benedictine nun. Other scholars, however, have objected to this assumption. The historical record and Julian's writings suggest more persuasively that Julian lived what was called in the fourteenth century a "mixed life" combining contemplation and prayer with the demands of the secular world. She was not a nun, though at midlife she sought to devote herself more completely to prayer and thus took a vocation that was open to laywomen: enclosure in an anchorage.

As for social class, Julian was most likely a member of the "parish elite"—neither aristocratic nor impoverished. In this role, she would have had opportunity both to seek out what education was available to a woman in sophisticated and dynamic Norwich and to develop close connections with the people of her parish, who would have come from a variety of social backgrounds. This is not the only conclusion that students of Julian's life can draw, but to my mind, it best suits the evidence we have.

While we may lack historical fact, we do have a rich, lingering material record of the fourteenth century to draw on. The people of England in the late Middle Ages were extraordinarily busy— war and plague aside—creating the world with their own hands. They left a remarkable record of their art and craftsmanship. Drawing on what we know of daily life, we can begin to trace the spiritual and cultural influences on an ordinary woman who was propelled from "unlettered creature," as Julian calls herself, to extraordinary theologian. Gathering together both material and theological understandings, we begin to picture her in the act of writing itself—an act at once so daring and so simple.

Prologue

ICTURE JULIAN. She sits at a plain oaken table in front of an upright writing desk with parchment attached to it by iron clips. She has brewed ink from crushed oak galls and rainwater, aged with an iron nail. The dark and murky liquid waits in a horn fitted to the desk. The parchment of finely scraped animal skin also waits.

For days, months, years, now even decades, she has been meditating on and crafting the words she will write on the parchment. Next to her, bound in leather, sits the first attempt that she made to tell her visions. She wrote it when her understanding was less full, when she had less courage, when her knowledge of words and their power and her trust in God's love were not as strong. This first attempt isn't wrong, but she has shaped its improvement through prayer, through long pacing across the reed-strewn floor. She has gained maturity and confidence in what God has shown her. Through the intervening years, accompanied by God's gift of unending love, she has shaped these words like a sculptor working over a body of clay, like perhaps God himself first formed humankind from the mud of the earth, giving his imagination form and then breath. That labor now behind her, she must shape the words on parchment without error.

I say "picture Julian," but how? We do not know what she looked like. We have several artists' renderings: a stern and studious Julian carved into the limestone entrance of Norwich Cathedral, standing across from St. Benedict with a book in her hand; or the sweet, upturned face of Julian imagined by the creators of more than one stained glass window. We have an elderly, almost ghostly Julian imagined by contemporary Australian painter Adam Oldfield. But as we read her six-hundred-year-old words, each of us creates a personal rendering of Julian that these images may not reach. And the problem is not only with visual images and versions: the scholarly rendering of her life and work is also conflicted.

Yet we can begin to step closer to Julian's mystery if we picture her at this writing desk. In one hand she holds a goose-quill pen, in the other, a penknife that can quickly scratch out mistakes and sharpen her quill when it becomes dull. Her first task is to record where and when her journey began, to say something carefully of the person she had been when the visions first came to her. She breathes deeply, checks the steadiness of her hand, focuses her mind just as she does for hours of prayer, and begins. This writing, too, is prayer.

JULIAN OF NORWICH
a contemplative biography

These revelations were shown
to a simple unlettered creature
the year of our Lord 1373,
the 13th day of May.

The First Window
THREE DESIRES

"This creature had once desired three gifts from God:
the first was minde of his passion;
the second was bodily sickness in youth;
the third was to have of God's gift three wounds."
A REVELATION, CHAPTER 2

THE CITY OF NORWICH. LENT, 1355.

THE RAIN CASCADED OFF THE EAVES OUTSIDE.
The clouds were thick and unyielding.

"*Benedicite,*" Julian said, kneeling in front of the priest.

"*Dominus,*" the priest answered.

Every year during Lent, Julian confessed at her parish church. Confessing only once a year was a difficult task for both parishioner and priest. The parishioner sorted through the many deeds and thoughts of the year past to extract those worthy of the attention of the priest. The priest listened for hours to common complaints, petty jealousies, secret burdens, and heartwrenching uncertainties. Both speakers needed to be comprehensive, so the soul could walk away unburdened;

and brief, because lines were long and neighbors impatient. Behind Julian, a crowd waited. Some muttered and clicked their rosaries, some chatted, others prayed.

Candles flickered and gave off a balmy smell of wax; the rain cooled the stone of unpaned windows.

"Have you had any envy to your neighbor or to your even Christians?" The priest led Julian through the seven deadly sins, sins of the five senses, and the dishonoring of the Ten Commandments. "Have ye been glad of her harms or her evil fare and loath of her good? Have ye backbited and disprised your even Christian or told evil tales of him to another?"

The priest urged Julian, a girl of twelve, to be more diligent in prayer, to remember her daily Paternoster and five Ave Marias, and to visit the sick more faithfully. After she rose from her knees, she lingered in the church in front of a painting of the crucifixion that depicted the women who had witnessed it gathered at Jesus' feet. Sometimes she felt as if the figures in the painting, so vivid their colors, might come to life. She wished that she could step into the painting and join them—to be with them and suffer with them. She lit a candle to Mary, who was almost as young as Julian when she became the Mother of God. After confession and devotion, she pulled her hood over her head and stepped out into the spring's wet.

She would do all that the priest asked of her, all that Holy Church taught. But sometimes she felt the priest was standing in her way, just a little. If he would move to the side, she thought, she might see God better. This was a thought she should confess. It was a sin of pride and a sin of impatience, but was it a sin to want to see God better?

As a child of the "common teaching of Holy Church," Julian attended mass daily, lifting her eyes to watch when the bell rang and the priest raised the host. On Sundays, she and her mother carried a basket of food to a neighbor whose hands had been crushed in a quarrying accident. Surrounded by her neighbors, she prayed before saints, danced in the parish hall, and ate the white round loaf of Eucharist once a year at Easter. She memorized psalms and the Hours of the Virgin, tried to discern her future sweethearts on St. Agnes Eve, joined the procession on Candlemas, and brought apples to be blessed on St. James's Day.

The ordinary life of the church came in bright colors, intimately made by the people's own hands. Vivid wall paintings, imaginative and witty corbels fitted at the joists of the church, and finely wrought stained glass told the sacred story that bound the people together. The parishioners lived together a deep common life, knowing intimately one another's welfare—whose bones ached in the cold, who had painful boils, who had been scalded as a child with malt. They knew about each other's marriages and children and relatives. With that kind of intimacy came the difficulties of individual personalities: gossipy neighbors, people who talked too loudly during the mass, those who drank too much, the self-righteous, the haughty, the mean-spirited. There would have been people she was eager to see when she went to church in the morning, and people she might secretly have hoped stayed home. Human character was sometimes, as Julian later writes, "good and gentle" and sometimes "cruel and oppressive."

The parish church was the center of life, and most parishioners believed in both God and the devil. They wanted to remember the saints' days and observe feasts and fasts as best they could. During daily mass, when only the priest partook of the bread and wine, they wanted him to hold the bread up high when he said, *"Hoc est enim Corpus Meum,"* so they could see it. They thought the end of the world was near and that they might assuage the wrath of God by giving to the poor and avoiding swearing. But their days were occupied with other matters as well. They bought bread and brewed beer. They wondered if the leather merchant was trying to cheat them. They fought with their neighbors over errant pigs and who was responsible for potholes on the street.

Though Julian learned from the church and saw it as her mother, she also came to want something more, something "beyond the common use of prayer." In this way, she was not an ordinary child, and as her faith formed, it contained a seed of longing for a closer vision, a deeper understanding, only—she later wrote—if it was within God's will. During her youth, Julian developed what she called in her writing "three desires." These desires are strange to modern understanding, but they would not have been extraordinary in her own day when life often centered around devotion to the church and ordinary piety contained hints of the mystical.

Her first desire was to have a "minde" of Christ's passion—a sensual recollection of what it would have been like to be with

Christ while he suffered on the cross. The second desire was a "bodily sickness" in which she would draw as close as possible to death's door without passing through it. The third desire was perhaps the most sophisticated of the three. She desired three "wounds," an idea that she picked up from hearing the story of St. Cecilia in church. She called the three wounds "contrition, compassion, and longing for God."

Julian's theology has its starting place in these three succinctly, if mysteriously, expressed desires. If we understand Julian's social and religious environment, the mix of spiritual and material that made up her everyday life, we can perhaps begin to understand what these desires meant to her and why she held on to them for so many years. They offer a small opening into the life of the young Julian.

JULIAN'S HOME CITY OF NORWICH THRIVED on the banks of the River Wensum. Its wealth came from its abundance of sheepwalks and production of wool. This far eastern part of England, called East Anglia, was located in close proximity to the North Sea. Trade with Zeeland, the Low Countries, and France accounted for its prosperity and sophistication.

Norfolk County dipped into boggy wetlands, rich with bird life, and then sunk farther into sandy, reedy sweeps of coastland. Agricultural and rural, it abounded in woodlands, grazing lands, and fields of wheat. Hawthorn and hazel, nettles, elderberry, foxglove, and oak dominated its intimate lanes and formed its ancient hedges.

By the time of Julian's birth in 1342, the city was six hundred years old. Early Anglo-Saxon immigrants built timber-framed houses, planted root vegetables and wheat. Danes brought knowledge of cheese and dairy production and made honey drinks. Normans imported wine and built massive stone monuments that directed and defined city life. Everyone raised sheep. The city was built in concentric circles radiating out from two central points: the castle and the cathedral, both built in the eleventh century following the French invasion of William the Conqueror. The French facilitated a long-lasting trade that brought people from all over the European world.

In Julian's early childhood, Norwich had a population of ten thousand. The second-largest city in England, it was growing fast. The wall around the city, made from local black flint stone and caulked with lime, had been finished the year of her birth, a proud symbol of self-sufficiency. Two imposing arches on either side of the River Wensum meant travelers knew when they had arrived to the city limits, and lines of carts snaked into the countryside every day as people waited to pay tolls to enter the city and join its marketplace.

Waking early to a morning mist, Julian would have heard the Angelus bell that signaled the end of the night watch. In the gray light, she heard the chatter of the first women on their way to draw water from the city wells, and the rattle and clang as butchers and blacksmiths welcomed first customers. In the churches, sleepy priests started mass early for travelers, workmen, and pilgrims headed out beyond the city walls. The noisy snuffles of pigs and lowing of cows filled the streets as children released animals from their pens and drove them out through the city gates to pasture.

After the first chores, but before breakfast, Julian left her house with her mother for church. They heard morning mass and offered their own prayers. Afterward they made their way to the market for the day's meat. Perhaps as they walked the streets, they saw boats and barges arriving from the port city of Yarmouth that carried sea coal, barrels of iron from Sweden, herring and onions, wood from Riga, Flemish lace, and light dry Rhennish wine, the color of sun through white curtains. The boats sent back fine wool, leather, latten, and wheat along with the proud products of the city's artisans—stained glass, intricately carved wood, illuminated manuscripts, and jewelry.

Goods arrived into port south of the city in an area called Conesford and came up the part-cobbled, part-mud Via Regina to the marketplace in carts and on sleds. Julian and her mother would have avoided this main thoroughfare and made a more convoluted route through the haphazard streets. Finer merchant homes stood tightly next to peasant cottages, tradesmen's workshops, and stone monasteries. Sometimes householders paved and maintained the streets; sometimes they left them to sink into pits of mud. Down the center of the streets ran a ditch into which people threw slop water and the remains of supper. Julian knew which streets to avoid, where butchers threw smoking animal entrails into the ditch and animals wandered unattended. She also learned to avoid the rayker, who from early morning started his route with a shovel, filling his cart with animal dung and refuse to carry outside the city walls.

But avoiding rank smells was impossible. Norwich was caught up in construction of new churches and chapels, along with thriving industries of dying, tanning, and fishing. Norwich stank of raw fish and acrid dye; the ripe scent of butchering and the dung-soaked hides of the tanneries added to a thick stew of human and animal stench: sweat, rotting standing water, lime, dripping animal tallow, and malt.

At church, the liturgy was recited in Latin, and in the marketplace, many of the merchants spoke French. But together, arm in arm avoiding puddles, Julian and her mother spoke English. English was a more carnal language than French or Latin, a language of the earth and of the body. Because it came from the countryside and from the people, some thought it impoverished and inadequate for expressing abstract thought. Yet England, now at war with France, had begun to assert its own identity, and the English spoken in Norwich would become the standard, a decade later, when the King made English the language of his courts. People were increasingly proud to speak English, and a certain disapproval had begun to creep into transactions conducted in French.

For Julian, English was primarily the language of home. With currents of Danish, Anglo-Saxon, Frisian, French, and Latin, this homespun English had never been formalized into a language of power. It had no set spellings or grammatical certainties. It was a language in use for practical purposes, constantly adapted to individual needs and contexts. In the evening after the curfew bell rang, people used English to tell stories and sing songs. English was the language of gossip; it was the language of the mystery plays that taught the lives of the saints. In English, a mother scolded her child, a child tended sheep, tanners shouted to each other across an alley. In other words, English was the language of the "lowly and simple things." For Julian, these limits eventually became a gift; in English she found a language that could exude both intimacy and power, a language in which the rules were not so well established that they couldn't be broken.

FOR MOST YOUNG PEOPLE, ONE TREK A DAY to church with their families would have been enough, but in Julian's young life, she sought out the church and its teachers often. She loved the muttering of the priests in chapels and the quiet that seeped in between masses. Franciscan friars often taught in the naves of local parishes, offering advice on prayer and meditation. While other young women shocked their elders with headdresses large enough to bump their neighbors in church and wobbly enough to look like they might topple, Julian likely wore a simple braid down her back and a linen shift, covered by a well-made woolen kirtle. Wealth could be conveyed through cloth, especially in a city whose prosperity rested on the wool trade. How silky your linen, how fine the weave of your woolen garments and its colors spoke volumes about your status. While Julian's clothes were sturdy and well made and the quality of the cloth reflected her father's success, these markings interested Julian less than the question of how to bring her heart closer to God.

For Julian, the preaching and teaching of the friars were her bread and butter. Her mother had taught her the basics of reading and writing. She had learned the creeds, the seven sacraments, and the orders of the angels. She knew the stories of many a saint's life. But she had few opportunities for more education, and she often felt restless, though she couldn't say for what.

In Norwich, friars of many different colored hoods abounded: Greyfriars, Blackfriars, Whitefriars. Each was connected to a specific monastic tradition, but they were freer than monks to reach out to common people and teach them. They offered sermons in their own yards, on street corners, and in local churches; they taught on morality, prayer, holy living, and salvation. They often read from the lives of the saints and offered instruction on how to keep the fasts of the church. A serious girl, Julian wanted to learn as much as she could. The most accessible teachers were the Franciscans. Franciscan teaching often focused on the crucifixion. The friars taught that one didn't seek revelation through prayer; one did not ask for special, secret messages from God. Instead, a person sought feeling, an alignment of the heart with God.

On a late spring day in Eastertide, when the sun shone brightly, the wind tormented the cloths drying at the tentagrounds, tied into frames. Julian prayed in her parish church, on her knees, practicing what she had been taught. Using her imagination to put herself as literally as she could at the foot of the cross, she tried to fill in details and truly feel what "Christ's lovers" might have felt. The images of Christ suffering, bleeding, and dying— sticky and oozing blood, flesh rent and sagging on nails—were supposed to open the heart to compassion, the friars said.

Julian wanted to free her heart to love Christ. To learn true contrition. To feel and not just speak her prayers. Yet, if she was truthful, she still meditated on Christ's passion and felt cold. Barren. Dry. A thousand questions pricked her. Perhaps she did not understand what the friars meant by feelings. Perhaps she had not yet discovered Christ's true compassion. In the flickering wax light, the "minde" of the Passion still seemed far away.

What if she just couldn't feel anything no matter how hard she tried? How, then, could she learn to love God better? She heard no answer in the friars' teaching.

ALL THAT SUMMER, Julian spent her time in the garden with the gardener. She asked him a dozen questions as she watched him pull turnips from the black soil and toss them into a basket. How did he know that the turnips were ready? How did he get them up without breaking the stems? What happened to the turnip if it got too big? Would he plant turnips in the same place next year or somewhere else? He wiped sweat from his forehead and wiped his hands on his mud-spattered tunic. He smiled a deep sun-and-wind-creased smile and laughed heartily at her questions.

At his instruction, Julian pinched insects off the chard leaves. She noticed that the gardener took all manner of things—scraps, peelings and cores, rotting things and putrid things. He turned them again into dirt. She watched him "delving and dyking and sweating" and "turning the earth up and down." She saw that he sought the right moment for planting and for watering, as he carefully watched both sky and earth. As he worked, the plants grew; their fruits formed. All that had been worthless and castoff was transformed into something valuable again. She carried his fruits to the kitchen in a basket.

In the kitchen, young Julian watched the cook preserve medlar and pippens. The cook added rock salt to the kettle and stirred with a wooden paddle. "You see," the cook held out her hand. "I put in about the size of a hazelnut for each batch." She helped to seal the fruit into clay jars for winter while a servant swept the earthen kitchen floor to spread new reeds mixed with artemisia and bay. The kitchen smelled damp and smoky, and the door stood propped open despite the flies. Parsnips rested in a barrel. Sausages hung curing from the ceiling. Fresh bronze-colored herring from the market were spread out on the table.

Meanwhile, the world outside arrived in strange and surprising ways. A peddler brought salted lemons by the house and sent one through the squint for everyone to try. A pilgrim spent the night in the family's yard and told of Veronica's veil, seen with his own eyes in Rome. He said that the face on the veil changed constantly, sometimes seeming to be gently gazing with love, sometimes appearing fierce, sometimes deathly, sometimes kindly. He showed them his prized badge from Walsingham, shaped from pewter into a tiny house.

AFTER THE HARVEST HAD BEEN BROUGHT IN and the days grew shorter and the light gloomier, Julian watched from her window as the priest made his way to the bedside of a sick neighbor. He came through the dark streets with an acolyte carrying a cross. The parish clerk went ahead, holding a lantern and ringing a little bell. The priest carried the sacrament at his breast in a small box as though cradling a child. The night air filled with the soft tinkling. "Hail! Light of the world, Word of the Father, true Victim, Living Flesh, true God and true Man. Hail flesh of Christ, let Thy blood wash my soul," the priest called out. The lantern light flickered against oilcloth shades hung over narrow windows. Inside, people rose from their beds and pulled on cloaks to begin a sleepy procession behind the priest to their neighbor's house.

Julian knew because she had seen it many times: the dying man would be reminded that the Mother of God would offer to all, even the most wayward, shrift and housel. He would be anointed and asked for his last confession. He would eat the *viaticum*, bread for the journey, offer his last wishes, and reconcile with his enemies so that he could walk free into the land beyond. If he died, the town crier would bring the news of his death with the end of the night watch.

What was that like for a dying person, Julian wondered, to cross the very last threshold of Holy Church into the realm beyond all that was known? Once the bread was eaten, the priest moved aside and ahead was only the country of God. Did the dying know something about God, she wondered, that everyone else could not know? Was the better sight and better feeling of God that she longed for on that side of life? Perhaps, as her mother said, she asked too many questions. It came to her mind, "freely without any effort," that she would like to have such a sickness so that she could know what lay beyond, in that far country where there were no longer any intermediaries between the soul and God.

IN NOVEMBER, after the trees had lost their leaves and the cold rains had begun, when all the grain was gathered in the cellar and her mother had counted and recounted the wooden barrels, hoping that they would feed the household for the winter, Julian and her mother went, as always, to church. That day, a priest told the story of St. Cecilia, a girl in ancient Rome whose family wanted her to marry. She objected, believing that God had a calling for her that was beyond the ordinary. But she was forced. On her wedding night, she converted her young pagan husband to Christianity and preserved her virginity. The two began to convert their friends and families. Word of their missionary zeal spread to the Roman authorities who killed Cecilia's husband and arrested her.

When she stood before the Roman provost, he asked her, "Know you not of what power I am?"

Julian thought Cecilia's answer shockingly but deliciously impolite as the priest read it out dramatically, "Your power is little to dread for it is like a bladder full of wind, which with the pricking of a needle is anon gone away and come to nought." The people around her snickered at the rude metaphor.

At that the provost ordered Cecilia's death, but when the soldiers tried to cut off her head they were thwarted by the power of God. They struck three blows at her neck, the most allowed by law, but mysteriously did not manage to kill her. She lived on for three days healing and saving many people.

The priest ended the story: "Let us devoutly pray unto our Lord that by the merits of this holy virgin and martyr, Saint Cecilia, we may come to his everlasting bliss in heaven."

"Amen," the people answered.

But it wasn't the everlasting bliss of heaven that stayed with Julian as she left the church and walked home in the bracing gray cold. It was the power in Cecilia's voice and the three wounds to her neck. She, too, wanted three wounds. Many years later, pen in hand, she named the wounds contrition, compassion, and longing for God. These were her spiritual desires. These were both the gifts and the wounds that she would earnestly seek her whole life.

The Second Window
THE TRAVAIL OF JULIAN'S YOUTH

"After this our Lord said:
'I thank thee for thy service and for
the travail of thy youth.'"
A REVELATION, CHAPTER 14

WHENEVER JULIAN ENTERED THE CHURCH, a scene of judgment and damnation spread out before her. There on the chancel arch in vivid reds and yellows, greens and blues was the Last Day. Tiny naked white sinners sent from God's throne to hell. Money lenders boiled in oil. Adulterers stripped and beaten. Grinning devils that dragged, prodded, and beat souls into hell. Christ sat above watching, unmoved.

One thing certain in the medieval church was that all human suffering was caused by sin and a punishment meted out by God on the unworthy. The suffering for sin began on earth, but carried on into the afterlife. Hell was the ultimate punishment, but purgatory was the destination of most souls not yet purified for eternal bliss. Purgatory was not a place where souls waited restlessly for heaven; it was not an empty sky. The soul had to be purged of sin, licked by flames. Punishments were fitted perfectly to sins: liars had their tongues sliced off; the gluttonous drank poison. The church fathers taught that the pains of purgatory far outweighed the pains experienced on earth. The dead remained connected, through prayer, to the living, who must continuously pray for them. Through prayer, these souls could move at last from purgatory to paradise.

BUT PREOCCUPIED AS PEOPLE WERE with eternal damnation and salvation, the hell that descended on Norwich during Julian's childhood and young adulthood seemed to have been handcrafted by God, not for the dead, but for the living.

The first occurrence of the "pestilence" came when Julian was a small child, just six years old. The plague arrived from the southwest of England after the season of Epiphany in 1349. Within a year, more than three quarters of the population of Norwich were dead.

For a child so young, the plague meant an entire world erased. At first, Julian listened to the wails, shrieks, and loss in her own house and in the houses of her neighbors. The tinkling bell that accompanied the priest to sickbeds sounded constantly. But then all bells ceased, as though time had simply stopped.

As the plague persisted, weary survivors piled bodies on their doorsteps. Outside the city, a huge open pit of decaying bodies grew, and its stench floated into the city on stiff spring breezes. Boats did not come into port. No one went to market. In the countryside, spring wheat went unplanted. If anyone managed to crawl out of their own homes toward church, they found their priests dead or gone. They whispered to each other that God meant to kill them all, as in the time of Noah, but they would have preferred the quickness of the flood to this slow and uncertain agony.

The plague lasted almost three years. Its devastation on Norwich, a crossroad of both trade and disease, was personal, social, and economic. No one was untouched by it. By the spring of 1352, when Julian was nine years old, few workers remained to collect trash and repair streets. No one rang bells or took animals out to pasture. Some survivors wandered aimlessly in what the city's leaders called "gangs of roving idlers." The king, whose fragile economy depended on the wool trade, ordered leaders to conscript these "idlers" into service for the city to repair its roads and bridges, to clean its streets, and to prepare the city to receive trade again.

Norwich tottered to its feet. Because disease, sudden death, and loss had become the ordinary, it felt strange to begin again. On the first morning that the Angelus bell rang again, Julian's mother rose, lit a fire, and urged her daughter to dress for church. On the way, her mother pointed to plants growing along the lane. "Look," she said, as though waking up from a dream. "The first hawthorn leaves are ready to be picked." A different ordinary life had to be restored. Gardens had to be cleared and then tilled and planted, streets recobbled, bridges repaired, the wall running up Carrow Hill rechalked. Life, impetuously, did return, at first in fits and then in waves.

THROUGHOUT HER YOUTH, THAT EARLY PLAGUE was like the memory of a nightmare to Julian. The outlines remained, but the specifics were vague. People spoke little of it, preferring to put their energy into restoring the lives they had had. If the plague had changed them, little evidence showed in daily life. Instead, people went about the necessary business of building a future. New people moved in to replace those who had died. A new candlemaker built a shop nearby, and Julian's mother thought him quite good. The new baker was less inclined to burn a loaf and sold a good one for a penny. The future now began to arrange itself. While we know nothing of the details, the outlines would have likely been ordinary: Julian grew into womanhood, married at her parents' behest, perhaps someone in the same trade as her father's, and by the time the second plague struck, was the mother of at least one child.

The year 1362, when Julian was nineteen, began with a sinister sign: the enormous steeple of the cathedral toppled in a galestorm. The wind of that storm was so strong that it crushed everything in its path. Waddle and daub houses crumbled; wooden market stalls tumbled in the streets; gates disappeared. But the greatest loss was the cathedral spire. It was the proudest symbol of Norwich. With the castle in disrepair, used now mostly to house unruly prisoners, the cathedral was Norwich's inspirational centerpiece. By sunrise on that winter morning, its impressive spire was rubble.

A few short months later, the pestilence struck again. This time, it had a new target: infants and small children. In her writing, Julian does not tell us of her own losses, whatever they might have been. Instead she offers a window into a time of terrible sadness. There was a time, Julian writes, "when I had a great longing and desire of God's gift to be delivered of this world and of this life. For oft times I beheld the woe that is here and the wellness and blessed being that is there. . . . This made me to mourn and earnestly to long—and also my own wretchedness and sloth and weariness—that I did not want to live and to travail as it fell to me to do."

At first, Julian and her mother visited every home in their parish. They washed sick bodies in vinegar and rosewater. They lanced the putrid sores and black buboes and then bound the wounds with tree resin and the petals of lilies. They made marigold and treacle ales and raised them to fevered lips. They kept vigils, lit candles, called on the help of saints. They helped their neighbors bury their dead until once again the losses were greater than their strength. Julian's face grew tight—first with fear, then with exhaustion, and finally with despair. Among the bodies in what she later called a "bloated heap of stinking mire" were those she loved best.

When she had been a small child, the grief and fear had been diffuse, like walking into a long fog. But now it was acute and it had a specific name: despair. Life became a long, dark tunnel. It wasn't that death was strange to her, not even unexpected. Yet at night, she startled awake thinking that she heard a child cry out and then did not sleep again for hours. During the day, she would pick up a basket of spinning and find herself, hours later, still holding the same bundle of wool in her hand. When people spoke to her, they seemed very far away and their voices indistinct. She reviewed each detail in her mind. She should have been with the children more. She forgot her Ave Marias the day that the youngest one died. Or she had been too selfish, too focused on her own loved ones when she should have been giving to others. She shouldn't have spoken so sharply to the cook. The littlest things made her grief rise with a force she did not think she could contain, remembering exactly how the sun had glanced across the floor when they had opened the first jar of currant jam last fall before all of this began. It startled her what her memory held and what it discarded. Every day, her children's faces seemed more faded, as if they were disappearing down a long dark hallway. She could remember clearly the day her son got sick, but nothing of the day just before it. Her memory deprived her of the happiest thoughts and left her a vivid recollection of misery.

Nearly everything she loved was now on the other side. All that remained here was woe.

THE SECOND ROUND OF THE PLAGUE split open the tiny questioning seeds of her youth. Pestilence was, the people of Norwich believed, God's work, but human sin played a role. People allowed themselves to be overtaken by their passions and in so doing, they opened themselves to miasmas, bad humors, and disease. Anger, lust, envy, and avarice opened the pores of the body, and evil scents and spirits that had both physical and spiritual attributes arose from stagnant water, muck heaps, and sewage. They could now enter the vulnerable body. But the correlation between sin and disease was not simple. Sin belonged to the whole community. Sin from one person's adultery could strike an innocent child. The whole body could be infected with the disease and sin of just one member.

For some, the pestilence was evidence of the *bellum Dei contra homines*—the war of God against humanity, waged because of human sin. In one sermon, given during a later plague, the preacher described the theology of the pestilence in a way that would have been utterly familiar to Julian. "God hath his quiver full of arrows, full of pestilence, fevers, all manner of diseases. He shoots them into our friends, our families, ourselves, and none but himself can pull them out." Some in Julian's community took it upon themselves to confess the sins of the whole community. They traveled in groups, flagellating themselves with whips and calling the people to repentance. The stink of the plague was as vivid evidence as they needed for the terrible odor of sin.

But for what sin had God chosen to bring the pestilence on them? The explanations offered by many of the priests, friars, and flagellants seemed laughable. Had God brought the pestilence because of drunkenness? Had entire villages been lost because of idleness? Had she lost her children because of the immoral way that some women dressed? The connection between righteousness and health had once made some sense to her. Had not Bridget of Sweden's son Karl died of his disordered, lustful passion? Could she not see the wages of sin on the bodies of the unrighteous? She had been taught that sin brought the devastating winds and rains, and it followed that sin brought the pestilence as well.

But now, she saw clearly that sin and pestilence had little correlation. The faithful and the unfaithful were both gone. The child and prostitute, clergy and parishioner, friar and laborer had all died without distinction. To try to make sense of such destruction only added misery to misery. The pain of living in the midst of her loss was already more than she could bear, and if she could follow the dead into the land beyond, she would.

Julian did not doubt the reality of sin. She could not deny the reality of suffering, but she could not imagine what purpose either might serve. She carried from the pestilence's devastation an irrevocable image of putrid and rotting flesh and a set of hard and seemingly unanswerable questions about God's grace. The greatest mystery was sin. Later she articulated the question this way: "Why was the beginning of sin not prevented?" Why allow it to infect every human being, every human community, every soul and every parish? Why let it fill the streets and houses with suffering without end? How could she persist in love, how could Christ persist in love with her, when she would sin and never be fully free from it?

The Third Window
MAY 13, 1373

*"He set the cross before my face, and said,
'Daughter, I have brought the image of thy savior.
Look upon it and comfort thyself.'"*
A VISION, SECTION II

FTER THE PESTILENCE, life refused to take its ordinary shape. Julian had always struggled to feel a life of faith as fully as the friars urged, but she now struggled to feel at all. She was often bored and restless. Little interested her. When she went to church and knelt every day, she felt like she was praying to the paint on the walls. Her own sin bothered her: What damage had her sin done in the world? How could God love sinful creatures? How could God forgive her? Sometimes she thought she could hear the words of her prayers pitched back to her in a mocking voice. The loss of both family and faith made everything seem dull and lifeless. The future stretched out bleakly—a long gray walk into darkness.

Yet, fortunately or unfortunately, the life of faith was not something that she could abandon. Holy Church and the communion of saints: this was her life's most basic currency. She could no more give up going to church, praying her rosary and saying the Paternoster upon rising than she could choose to stop breathing. And even more than these practices, which could be emptied of all feeling, something else remained like a very small light in the darkness: what she later called "love-yearning," her basic desire for God that could not be rubbed away. She kept a habit from childhood. Whenever the pain of despair or of impatience became too great, she practiced saying, "As is God's will," even if she had to say it without feeling.

Often she felt lonely. Many of the people of her parish continued on as before: they prayed to the saints, lit candles for their dead, and then went out and negotiated a better price for their cows' milk. Julian could not reconcile the God who had so cruelly brought the pestilence with the God she prayed to in the great compassion of the crucifixion. If she was being asked to live through this strange travail, was there someone who might help her?

Almost ten years passed. Julian was now thirty years old, living with her mother. After May Day in Eastertide, she fell suddenly ill. On May Day, dancing and feasting had lasted late into the night. The parish hall was richly decorated with primroses and morning glories woven into wreaths. The women had made green pudding and green beer to celebrate the coming of spring. A few days after these celebrations, Julian did not get up from her bed. She complained of a loss of feeling in her limbs, and her fever was high. Her mother made compresses of yarrow and brewed lemon balm tea, but the fever worsened. For three days she suffered, and at last her mother called the curate to give Julian last rites. The curate made the solemn procession with a neighbor boy serving as acolyte. Dressed in a black robe, the priest asked Julian for her confession and anointed her with oil from the small silver flask he carried. "Believest thou fully that Christ died for thee and that thou may never be saved but by the merit of Christ's passion?" he intoned.

"Yea," she answered.

"In manus tuas commendo spiritum meum," he muttered in a low chant and administered the bread from his tiny pyx. Then he and the little boy went away.

A few days later, May 13, 1373, before dawn Julian was still alive. Her breath had become ragged. She asked her mother to help her sit up to ease her breathing. With the help of a neighbor woman, she pulled Julian up and arranged the hemp-covered pillows and bolsters to support her. Then she sent the neighbor to ask the curate to come again.

Was she meant to live? Julian's eyes fluttered to the oak-beamed ceiling of the room and fixed there. Julian wondered what the will of God would be. Later she wrote that dying at such a young age had seemed to her then a sad waste. But in dying, she also felt she would be delivered from suffering to bliss. Her thoughts were feverish and restless. Her prayer formed, as was her habit, a question: "May my living no longer be to thy glory?" She determined to keep her eyes on heaven until she knew the will of God.

When the priest bustled into the room, again with the little boy, she was vaguely aware of his presence, but she did not move her eyes from the ceiling. The priest moved closer to her bedside and held the large metal cross just inches in front of her face.

"Daughter," she heard him say, with a command in his voice. "I have brought the image of thy savior. Look upon it and comfort thee therewith."

For a long moment, while the priest cleared his throat, Julian did not lower her eyes to the cross. It seemed to her, she wrote later, that her eyes were "well as they were." Trained on heaven, she would discern God's will. That old feeling of the priest being in the way had stayed with her. Hadn't he already done his work? She had given her confession. He had administered last rites. Why was he here? She did not want to know God's will by the cross or by the priest or by any "intermediary."

Then she reconsidered. Why had she refused to look at the cross? Perhaps this was stubbornness. Perhaps she needed to submit to Holy Church more fully than she had. Perhaps if she lowered her eyes to the cross that the priest held so insistently in front of her face she might live a little longer and understand God's will a little better.

With effort, she lowered her eyes and tried to focus them on the cross that the priest held in his hand. At first, her eyes burned from having been fixed on one spot for so long. Gradually, she noticed that her sight appeared to be failing. The room was darkening, as if a cloud had passed over the sun. Then it seemed that night was falling, and as she continued to watch, the room plunged into a darkness deeper than she had ever known. It was a haunted, demon-filled darkness. The only thing illuminated in the room was the cross. A common light shone on it, like sunlight through a window. But she could not say what its source was.

"This is death," she thought, as the lower part of her body started to lose feeling, and life seemed to drain from it. She could not breathe; a great weight lay on her chest and soon would squeeze out her breath.

And then, in an instant, everything changed. The pain that had preoccupied her for days went away, like the lifting of a curtain. Then the cross that the priest held in front of her face started to bleed. The blood trickled from the crown of thorns around Jesus' head and then began to run hot and thick. It flowed "like water off of the eaves of a house after a great shower of rain," "like the scales of herring," like "pellets" of grain. The image was "alive and active, hideous and dreadful, and sweet and lovely" all at once. She could almost smell the metallic sourness of the blood and feel its stickiness.

The blood flowed so continuously that she thought, "Surely it will soak the bed." And then looking more closely, she saw that the blood flowed from Christ's head but did not fall.

A voice spoke in her vision and said, "With this, the Fiend is overcome."

As the cross came alive, she saw that she was watching Christ die. She thought he looked like a piece of leather left out drying in the sun. The nails twisted his flesh, and the weight of his body became terrible. She saw the thorns and the flesh clinging to them as it was torn away. Hair, dried blood, skin, bones, pieces of flesh hanging from thorns, his wounds gaping holes. "If I had known the pain," she later wrote, "I would not have asked for an understanding of it."

Then she heard another voice that said to her, "Look up to heaven." It sounded like a friendly voice, and she considered its request. By looking up to heaven, she could escape this terrible suffering. She paused.

"No," she said. "I cannot."

In that instant, she chose Jesus over the bliss of heaven. She chose to stay with him no matter how long his suffering lasted. She would not escape from the suffering, as she had longed to escape during the worst days of the pestilence and in its aftermath. She would stand with Jesus and choose him—his blood, his flesh, his misery—for her heaven. And she would not do this out of dreary obligation, but out of love.

Of the three desires that she had expressed in her youth, all of them were fulfilled in this vision, at once terrible and lovely. She had more of a "minde" of the Passion than she had known was possible. She'd indeed experienced the bodily sickness that had propelled her into a new landscape, and her longing for God so completely overtook her that her heart split wide with compassion. At one startling moment in her vision, Jesus looked at her from the cross and said, "Lo, how I love thee." And for one equally startling moment, she believed him.

The Fourth Window
"I HAVE BEEN RAVING"

"'This man takes seriously the least word that I could say.'"
A REVELATION, CHAPTER 66

OR MANY HOURS, JULIAN REMAINED in the realm of her visions. She spoke at length with God, saw many signs, and heard many words "formed in her understanding."

She called out *"Benedicite Dominus"* over and over again. Once, she said out loud, "Today is my Doomsday," and another time she laughed merrily, even joyfully. Her eyes were wide and strange, and those in attendance could not reach her with ordinary words or questions. In between these outbursts were hours of silence.

The priest took his leave, but Julian's eyes had been so trained on the cross that he left it propped at the foot of the bed. The hours passed. Julian's mother stood and stretched, paced the room, took up some tatting, put it down again, returned restlessly to her daughter's side to see if she still breathed. A woman brought a bowl of nettles soup to her. Another idly swept the room. The bells rang for evensong, compline, curfew.

Now in the middle of the night, the room was lit by tapers. The evening's fire had smoldered and ashed, and a neighbor woman placed a shawl around Julian's mother's shoulders. The silence was deep, except for the night watchman who called out every hour with the chiming of his bell.

Julian's mother came up to her daughter's bed and leaned in close. She paused but did not hear that now-familiar ragged breath. She did not see her daughter's chest rise and fall. Julian's eyes were still rigidly open. Her daughter must, then, at last be dead. She reached out to close Julian's eyes.

Julian, however, was not dead. Deep in the midst of the visions, she had been watching Jesus' body dry on the cross. She had seen the "wrenching of the nails and the weight of the body." The wind howled, stingingly cold. Julian felt the pain, "recollecting" now fully the passion of Christ, the gift for which she had asked long ago.

When her mother reached over to close her eyes, her hand blocked the vision. Julian could no longer see Jesus on the cross. Even though the pain of Christ's suffering was so much she thought it might kill her too, still Julian longed to see it more than she wished to be freed from it. The vision of Christ on the cross somehow shared the same space in the room as mother and neighbors and servants. It was there with the loom and the embroidery screen, the slop bucket and the wash basin. *I am not in pain*, she wanted to tell her mother, though she could not speak. *It is only Christ's pain in me.*

THE HAND THAT JULIAN'S MOTHER HELD in front of Julian's face was marked by hard work. Roughened and reddened, wrinkled and veined; a thick callous on the middle finger where the hand had held an embroidery needle for many hours. The fingernails blunt cut with a knife. A hand whose creases were known and loved, a hand homely and familiar.

Julian's writing leaves us this trace of her mother: her hand. The two women had no doubt shared a great deal together. They had walked their family through death, not once, but several times. They had served together, prayed together, eaten many a meal of maslin bread dipped in soup, and spent many hours by the fire. They had shared the trial of the pestilence together, taken turns at neighbors' and children's bedsides, studied each other's faces carefully every morning for traces of the sickness, though they saw only weariness. They had tested each other's patience, had moments of conflict, and they intimately knew each other's faults.

In this moment, Julian's mother blocked Julian's view of Jesus. No matter the tenderness or sadness or impatience in her gesture, she was standing, literally, between Julian and Jesus. As Julian walked out into the landscape of God, the person nearest to her, the mother whose "service is nearest, readiest, surest," not only could not go with her, but stood in her way. She had to go alone.

WHEN JULIAN RETURNED TO CONSCIOUSNESS, day-
light was already old. The market was closing. Workers headed
to alehouses, and on the street, the smell of the mutton
pie bakers momentarily overtook the smell of the fish sellers.
Julian's head began to ring as though full of bells—not ringing
as a call to prayer but a terrible noise without meaning. Then
she felt all the pain in her body as before—legs, lungs, head.
With the pain came desolation. The connection to Jesus that
she had just experienced was real; she could still hear him say,
"Lo, how I love thee." But what good was it if she had to still be
here in this miserable flesh? Back in the body, in its pain and its
limitations, she felt petulant and annoyed.

Opening her eyes gradually, she looked around at the room—
the flint-lined fire pit, the washbasin with a rag hanging over the
side, a cup of now-cold ale. She looked down at the dun-colored
blanket that covered her legs and felt as if she was looking into a
vast desert. This life had no more to offer than emptiness. How
could she hold on to the consolation of that other world? She
panicked in fear of forgetting. The other world was receding, and
she could not cling to it. Everything hurt, especially the fact that
she was left here in this life alone.

But she was not alone in the room after all. A man sat on a
stool next to her, his head with its familiar bald tonsure bent
as if in prayer; his black robe spilled onto the floor. This was

not the priest who had been with her earlier with his bustling officiousness. This man's presence was so quiet, so gentle that she was long in sensing it and longer in acknowledging it. When he saw that she was awake, he took her hand and held it. His hand was rough from long hours of gardening; his face was already brown from spring planting. He smiled. "How do you fare?" he asked.

"I have been raving," she said with an edge of bitterness in her voice and pulled back her hand. Then she laughed and surprised herself to hear the laugh that came out. It was unfairly bitter, she thought, and wished she could take it back. He laughed too, but there was something uncertain in his laugh, a question more than an answer.

His eyes searched hers for understanding. She wondered if she could tell him the truth.

"That cross," she said gesturing to the foot of the bed where the curate had been. "That cross that stood before my face, it seemed to me that it bled fast." She paused, wondering if she should go on.

The man's face changed. It turned serious.

His surprise startled her. "This man takes seriously every word I say. He does not think I am mad." She felt a sinking sensation of shame. Why had he paid such close attention when she mentioned the bleeding cross? Should she tell him more? But how could she tell it to any priest? Who would believe her? He would only laugh at her. A woman, seeing things.

Before they could talk further, others in the room noticed that Julian was awake. They chased the man from her bedside. She felt stung by the shame she had felt when she had seen his eyes. In her visions, she had been overtaken by compassion. Love had personally entered the room and spoken to her. And then because of a little bodily pain upon waking, she was ready to dismiss it as "raving." God had answered her prayers, and her response to this tremendous love was to laugh. She had been afraid that the man would laugh at her, but in fact, she had mocked Christ.

She would confess this sin now, if she could, just to be relieved of it. But how could she confess it? Once she told a priest, any priest, he would tell her she was a silly child, that she should go back to her Paternosters and ask God to calm her mind. She thought of her curate who had brought the cross to her face. He did not wish to know the inner ravings of her mind. He wanted her to be good, to perform acts of service, come to mass, believe on Jesus, and not make his burden for her salvation too heavy. Between them was an unspoken agreement. He would do his duty, and she would do hers. For many years, this silent understanding between Julian and her priest had been unsatisfying. She craved more: a better understanding of God and God's will. But she had long known not to ask her many questions to her priest. She knew that he certainly would wish to hear nothing of her visions.

But this other man, this friar, who had come to see her and sat by her bed: could he hear her?

The thought that he might hear her made her suddenly afraid. He lacked cold formality, this priest. Instead of demanding something of her, he had *asked* how she fared and seemed genuinely, surprisingly interested in the answer. When she laughed, he laughed. But when she dismissed her visions as "raving," he had been startled. She wished he would come back so that she could make better sense of his eyes.

INSTEAD, HER HEAD ACHING, she drifted into a troubled sleep. As she tossed and turned, yet another man appeared at her bedside. This one infiltrated her sleep. He was the devil, she could tell, hot and stinking. He thrust his face—red with black spots—into her face, his teeth long, white, and ugly. He blew stinking breath onto her. He set at her throat, wanting to strangle her. His hands were like paws clawing at her.

"*Benedicite Dominus!*" Julian called out. "Is all on fire here?" The room seemed to be consumed in flames.

"Nay. There is no fire. Rest."

"Blessed be God," she called out. "It is the devil come to assail me."

As a loud and impatient screeching filled her ears, Julian tried to drown out the noise with the prayer she had repeated every day of her life. "*Pater Noster qui es in caelis: sanctificetur nomen tuum.*" She recited the liturgy of the Passion and the creed, every word that she had ever learned in church, but the devil stayed with her, incessant, cruel, demanding.

WHEN, IN THE MORNING, HER MOTHER opened the curtain to let the warming air in, the devil was gone. Still smelling his stench, Julian remembered the last words that Jesus had said to her.

> Know it well.
> It was no raving that thou saw today,
> Take it and believe it.
> Keep thyself in it and comfort thyself with it
>   and trust thyself to it.
> And thou shalt not be overcome.

Julian at last fell into a peaceful sleep, but as she drifted off, she laughed. In her visions, Christ had told her: The devil is nothing. Sin is nothing. His torments are nothing. Now she saw that it was true. For all the time that she had spent worrying about sin, imagining how much pain her sin had caused, she saw that sin was nothing. The devil himself had come to torment her and had not been able to harm her. She almost felt pity for sin and its worthlessness. "Poor, wretched sin. What art thou? Thou art nought. When I saw that God is all things, I saw thee not. When I saw that God has made all things, I saw thee not."

Something had been healed, an old and ugly wound. The personal attack by the devil allowed her to see and to smell the difference between good and evil. She now knew how God reached her with "secret touching" and gentle wooing, and how the devil came in vicious, but impotent, attack.

When she woke again, hours later, her mother came to her with a cup of warm ale. Julian realized that Jesus had left her no sign, no token by which she could know what all of this meant. How would she ever understand what had been shown to her?

The Fifth Window
THE FRIAR

*"The constant seeking of the soul
pleases God very much."*
A REVELATION, CHAPTER 10

S JULIAN RECOVERED from her illness, the city of Norwich was also in the midst of a dramatic recovery. After dipping to a population of five thousand from a height of thirty thousand, the city was beginning to rebuild. New construction dotted lanes and streets. The marketplace was repaved and the docks newly timbered. The guilds recruited members, and merchants took up a collection for a new church to replace the ancient one at St. Peter Mancroft. The city's leaders organized the buying of property so that they could have better control over sanitation, the removal of garbage, and the placement of paving stone.

Ironically, the death of so many in the plague had cleared much-needed space for fresh energy to flow in. *Regimen Sanitatis,* an old document about good living, gained new adherents for its advice on proper diet, exercise, and healthful behavior. It urged, and the city's leaders listened, that near residential building there "be no evill sents of puddle-water or of excrements." Ordinances for the disposal of water used in dyeing and tanning, proper disposal of animal remains and waste, and the containment of livestock began to take effect, giving people a new sense of order.

English-speaking laborers came into the city from the countryside, and new craftsmen built workshops along the ancient streets. Norwich became newly famous for its orchards and gardens. The monks at the cathedral began to work on plans for a roof that would be made of York stone and lead instead of wood. They worked continuously on the completion of the cloister and commissioned misericords for the choir. Craftsmen developed new colors for stained glass and dyes for cloth. Since Norwich's wool trade was heavily promoted by the king, new weavers and new dying and mixing techniques came to the city from Flanders and Zeeland. Dornix—a blend of wool and hemp—was woven into exquisite floral patterns and hung in the flapping breeze at the marketplace. Worsted wool that came from a special sheep bred in Norfolk made a smoother fabric that positioned Norwich for future prosperity.

CHANGES, THOUGH NOT ALL POSITIVE, were underway in other regions of England as well. Edward III had been in power for almost five decades and was now ill and scandal ridden. His mistress had been banished from the court for holding too much power over the weakened king. In 1377 he died, some said of syphilis, and his ten-year-old grandson, Richard II, became king. For a time, the kingdom shuddered with uncertainty, as the young king's uncle, John of Gaunt, assumed greater power. Many wondered if he would take the throne for himself.

The church hierarchy, too, was in turmoil. Two popes claimed apostolic succession, one in Rome and one in the French city of Avignon. In Rome, cardinals elected Pope Urban VI in 1378, and some quickly discerned his election as a mistake. He was impulsive and easily angry. The people around him accused him of lacking gentleness and charity. All of this might have been tolerated had he not also begun lecturing the cardinals in arrogant tones about their practice of accepting gifts in exchange for political favors.

The cardinals, especially the French cardinals, decided to hold another election. They chose Robert of Geneva as their pope. He took the name Pope Clement VII and established a rival court in Avignon. Since neither pope had a particularly strong character and they differed little in theology, preference for one pope over another became a question of culture and geography. England had been at war with France for almost fifty years, and the English declared undying loyalty to Pope Urban.

To add to the turmoil, in London a priest named John Wycliffe, a friend of John of Gaunt, set the church hierarchy on fire with a searing critique. He saw the church in desperate need of reform. Like Urban, he argued that clergy should not be in the habit of accepting gifts from the wealthy and that the church had become too dependent on its political alliances while the people struggled and starved. He urged the church to withdraw from politics and leave ruling to the king. Poverty, not luxury, should be the mark of holiness. While speaking out about church politics, Wycliffe was also diligently translating the Gospels into the commoners' English because "it helpeth Christian men to study the Gospel in that tongue in which they know best Christ's sentence." This was an idea so radical it reverberated across England for a century, setting the stage for the Reformation.

BUT IN NORWICH, WYCLIFFE'S TEACHING and the papal schism had little immediate effect. Before he died, Edward III had appointed Henry Despenser bishop of Norwich, and he would remain in power throughout Julian's life, dictating the limits of reform and keeping the church well in line with the old hierarchies. Despenser was the son of a very old, noble family. Unlike Wycliffe, he had no problem with the entanglement of church and kingdom; he was the wealthy son of both.

Arrogant and demanding, Bishop Despenser was also an intensely loyal person. By the end of his career, he was best known, even infamous, for acts of extreme loyalty to those to whom he considered himself obliged. His participation in the crusades, his role in crushing the peasant uprising of 1381, and his execution of followers of Wycliffe, called the Lollards, make his legacy a bloody one, but all of his acts can be traced to a passionate loyalty to king and church.

JULIAN PROBABLY PAID LITTLE ATTENTION to Bishop Despenser as she emerged out of her illness into ordinary life. He had yet to spend any time in Norwich, and she did not know, at that moment, that he would have any effect on her life. Instead, she was preoccupied with her visions. If the pestilence had chastened Julian and the visions awakened in her a profound compassion, she now felt a deep longing for God, as if that small flickering "love-yearning" had become a steady flame. Her encounter with the Christ of the crucifixion gave her the courage to reach out for help. In a state of hungry curiosity and hope, Julian decided to find the friar who had been at her bedside.

Julian was familiar with many of the friars and friaries in Norwich. She had often gone to hear sermons preached by them; she had attended festivals and marched in procession with them. In general, she had found, friars did not view women as church servants, as priests often did. Instead, they frequently engaged them in informal relationships. She herself had learned a great deal from the friars throughout her life, and even begun to build tentative friendships with a few.

Julian could be sure, as she walked along the cobbled stone toward Conesford Street stepping out of the way of carts, that she could seek out a male spiritual advisor without incurring too much scandal. She had to be careful about appearances and keep careful watch on boundaries. But it wasn't unusual or impossible for a woman to engage in a relationship with a "religious" who could be her helper, counselor, and teacher. She could ask him to be her confessor, go to him for the absolution of her sins, and then, if he was willing, she could ask him the many questions that were on her heart.

For most of Julian's life, she had been guided by Franciscan friars. She had admired that they offered ordinary people a way to make Christian teaching intimate. They turned no one away and invited people to participate vividly and imaginatively in the stories they taught. Julian felt anxious about leaving them behind as she went to look for a new teacher, but she knew that the Franciscans were skeptical of mystical visions. Instead of receiving revelation, they wanted people to be emotionally engaged in prayer, just the sort of prayer that Julian felt had been failing her—or she it—for many years.

Today, as the brisk autumn wind picked up from the southeast, she was determined to walk a little farther down the road and inquire at the Austin Friary on Conesford Street. The Austin friars, called the Friar Hermits of St. Augustine, had more learning than the Franciscans. One of them had studied in Italy under Catherine of Siena, whose mystical visions had electrified Rome. Julian had gone many times to hear these friars preach; she had been drawn to their learnedness. It made sense to return there now.

She hoped to find the friar she was looking for at St. Michael's, the large new flint stone church at the gate of the monastery. The friars' work there, other than study and gardening, was a daily round of masses said in memory of the dead. She hoped she might find the friar saying a mass, so that she could speak to him without making too much of a spectacle of her desire.

Julian approached the Austin friary and entered nervously through the great wooden door of St. Michael's church. There, in the flickering light, she took a deep breath. The earthen floor strewn with reeds and the soft thatch overhead gave the church a damp smell and a deep quiet. She looked around and saw no one she knew. She asked a young boy sweeping out the nave for the friar. He told her to wait, and she did, anxiously, pausing before a statue of Mary to light a candle and say a prayer.

It seemed ages before the boy returned. She considered going home. It was a fool's errand anyway. If the friar did appear, she would simply thank him for coming to see her while she was ill and then go quickly away. But she had vowed to be true to her visions, not to turn away from them in fear, as she had done before. She coaxed herself at least to say a word, however small, of her hope and let him answer.

When the friar came out, she recognized his smile. His immediate warmth surprised and unguarded her. He ushered her to a side chapel, and she told him, keeping her voice as steady as she could, of her errand. She wanted him to be her confessor. She knew that he was busy, that he had much work at the friary and with his studies, and people found his preaching most helpful. But if he might find a little time for her, she would be grateful.

He interrupted her. He would be honored. He had been thinking a great deal about her bleeding cross and was very glad that she had come to speak with him. He wanted to hear more. He thought that she should come the following week, perhaps after nones. Since the light was still good, she should be able to get home before dark.

All the way home, Julian breathed in the excitement. The daring. The risk of it. How, after all that she had seen, could she have doubted that God would open a way for her to learn? She ached to see how close she now came to that which she most desired. It felt as if the sky had split open and blessings were raining down on her.

The following week, she prepared herself for their meeting with a long time in morning prayer. She tried to allow the excitement to exist alongside the steady rhythm of her heart. Then, after a meal with her mother, she again walked toward St. Michael's, breathing and repeating to herself, "As is God's will."

The friar did not at first speak of the bleeding cross, and Julian was reluctant to mention it. Instead, the friar began by teaching her the practice of *lectio divina*. He gave her a small piece of Scripture, at first only a few words, translated it for her from Latin, and showed her how it could be read, memorized, and meditated on until it became as intimate as a part of her body, as if she had eaten it. Once she became adept in this practice, he copied out longer passages for her to carry home so that she could study between their meetings.

Then, one afternoon, the light now weaker as winter approached, he asked her to tell him everything that she had seen the day that the cross bled. She had rehearsed many aspects of her visions over and over in her mind, but she expressed to him her nagging fear that she would forget the visions and that she had not understood the most important parts. He sat for a long time in silence after that, as though turning over a thought in his mind, unsure whether he should speak it. Then he said, "Remember what you have learned of the *lectio divina* and use it to bring these visions closer to you."

The next week, he came to their meetings with a small scroll with a few chapters of Paul's letters to the Romans. He said, "Your questions are on the nature of sin and grace. I believe that we should begin to look more carefully at the writings of blessed St. Paul."

He unrolled the scroll and began to translate for her from Latin. "Are we to continue in sin that grace might increase? God forbid! How shall we who died to sin still live in it?" She carried that precious scroll home with her and hid it in her knitting basket. Then she began the practice of walking, praying, and asking to understand. She layered what the friar taught her with what Christ had told her in the visions.

All of her life, the people around her had been impatient with her incessant questions—the priests, the Franciscan friars, her mother, the gardener. But now for the first time in her life, she felt free to ask, free to wrestle, free to struggle. The love of Christ that she carried with her from the visions combined with the willingness of a patient teacher meant that she came to see her questions in a new way. She wasn't being impudent or rude or sinful when she asked for understanding. The friar told her that God wills our wrestling, but that God wasn't satisfied with wrestling alone. "God wills our understanding. God wills that we ever more and more be fulfilled," he told her. "God does not loathe your questions, daughter, but treasures them. He will give you more insight as you are ready."

Week by week, as winter turned into spring and back again toward summer, the friar offered his teaching to his hungry student. Perhaps he was unaware that he was giving her the tools that would lead her to tell her own story. But he offered her what he had, and then stepped quietly into the shadows, not seeking attention for himself.

The Sixth Window
MIXED LIFE

"Our Lord has oned us together in love."
A REVELATION, CHAPTER 78

T HE VISIONS HAD CREATED A RADICAL BREAK. Julian did not know what they meant or what to do with them, but she knew that her life would be forever measured in before and after. At first she clung to the images and ideas that had emerged from her visions on the sickbed. She tried desperately to fix them in her mind through repetition. But as she meditated on them, using what the friar had taught her of *lectio divina,* she realized something astounding: they did not end. The visions were not so much an event that had come out of her illness as they were an ongoing reality to which she could nearly always have access in prayer. Now that that reality had broken through the screen of her fears and "doubtful dread," she saw them again and again. She was not responsible for retaining the visions, as if they were a few precious handfuls of grain that would soon be used up. Instead, they flowed like the blood of Christ, mysteriously, continuously, and "plenteously."

Life took on new dimensions. She continued to attend church with her mother. Together they made ales for church festivals, embroidered linen for the altar, and spent Sundays on their regular round of parish visits. In her rounds to hear the many preachers and teachers who passed through the parishes of Norwich, Julian discovered other women similarly interested in becoming serious students of prayer. Together they met to say matins. They gave one another prayers and votive drawings to tuck into their prayer books. A little at a time, she disclosed to them what she had seen, and sometimes they used her visions as a starting place for their own contemplation. They became a small circle of "lovers of God," devoted to aiding one another in a prayer-directed life.

Together this circle began to live what came to be called a "mixed life": they became seriously devoted to prayer and yet stayed outside the convents, still responsible for their families and communities. In previous centuries, a woman in Julian's position would have had to choose the convent or marriage. Common people were expected to be devout, but they were not considered to be "religious," a calling that brought with it status and opportunity, as well as safety and the necessity of obedience. But in Julian's day, the possibility that someone could be "religious" without being "a religious" was just beginning. This path came to be called mixed life or, in Middle English, *medled lyf*, and it contained elements of both devotion and secularity. Many people, not only those in monasteries, were hungry for prayer, and they were encouraged by the friars to deepen their commitments in ways that were not unlike those found in monasteries. Many of those seeking mixed life were women, married or widowed; like Julian they had spent their lives in the church, always believing that nuns had taken the superior path. But might there not be ways that ordinary people could learn to love God better?

As Julian devoted more time to prayer and contemplation, an odd thing began happening. The "showings" became a conversation, even a dialogue. She could clearly discern the voice of Jesus the way she had experienced it during her illness, without the moving of lips, as "words formed in her understanding." She found that she could speak to Jesus, ask questions, and receive answers. Not only that, but her questions could be bold, challenging, disbelieving, or even angry, and she would still receive some kind of answer. The voice that guided her was courteous and unfailingly kind. She often felt stupid and stubborn as she challenged him, but he remained patient. She considered well the questions that she asked, knowing that the asking itself was daring. She wanted to be sure that she was not asking for special knowledge, only to know "lowly" and "ordinary" things that could be shared with others.

Especially, she wanted to understand sin better, since it had long been a puzzle to her. In her original visions, she had heard God say, "All shall be well, all shall be well, all manner of all thing shall be well," but such a saying made no sense to her. "Good Lord," she asked, "how can all be well considering the great damage that has come through sin to Thy creatures?"

His answers were difficult to understand and required still more meditation. Sometimes she was shown secrets that she knew were meant for everyone. Other times she glimpsed a deeper mystery that provided no way inside itself. She came to call this "the Great Deed," that which will be understood only in God's own time. The showings—the revelations—were like mysteries within mysteries within mysteries. She saw that even while she gazed at Jesus on the cross, when he was with her in that way that she called "bodily sight," she still longed for him. The seeing and the seeking did not separate from each other. She could "possess" Jesus in this way and still "lack" him. At first, she found this frustrating. She wanted the feeling of seeking to give way to satisfaction. But eventually, she understood that this was the very condition of human life: to possess some knowledge of God and yet always to be failing. To be in an intimate relationship and yet still feel the distance. In this way, faith could be cultivated instead of demanded. In "seeing" and "seeking," love flourished.

so true

The church had taught her that confusion was a sign of the devil's work, and at first she feared the bewilderment that she felt when she pondered her visions. She worried that if she expressed her confusion and doubt, she was saying, in essence, that she could not discern the devil's voice from God's. She knew that the devil cast doubt on the very pillars of the soul and caused them to tremble. She had experienced this doubt many times herself. But as her prayers deepened, she realized that discerning Jesus' voice from the devil's was the simplest mystery she faced. The devil's voice sneered at her. "Thou knowest well that thou art a wretch and a sinner, and also untrue. Thou oftentimes promise the Lord that thou shalt do better, and immediately afterward fall into the same. Thou art especially guilty of sloth and wasting of time." The devil's voice went on and on, accusing her and whining at her in a tone she might once have thought worthy of her attention.

Jesus, she learned, never spoke to her like this. His tones were always gentle. He did not accuse or blame. She knew that her visions were from God, and yet quite often they were baffling. He had filled the landscape of prayer with a great number of mysteries and secrets. But the two kinds of bewilderment—the confusion wrought by the devil and the delightful mystery of God—could not possibly be more different.

The church's teaching about the confusions of the devil was just one of the ways that she struggled to make sense of the church to which she was devoted and in which she had been raised. The church and her visions seemed, at least on the surface, frequently at odds. It was never her intention to challenge the faith of her childhood. Yet often the church's teachings and the revelations she received seemed to conflict. In her visions, Christ put no emphasis at all on evil. She had asked to see hell and purgatory, and she had seen nothing. Even the damned, as were painted on the church wall, had not made an appearance in her revelations. Why were church teachings and the revelations so different? To imagine that Christ had shown her something outside the church was a thought almost too terrible to think.

Eventually Julian came to an understanding by which she was "somewhat eased." The church offered a set of teachings like a ceilinged room, while her visions were as vast and broad as the sky. The sky contained and enclosed the ceilinged room, just as the room contained and enclosed her. She saw that she could in no way leave the ceilinged room—it was her home as much as the sky. At the same time, her knowledge of the sky could help her to understand the room better.

One night she was again wrestling with the question of sin. She saw that she sinned and that all people sinned, grievously, endlessly. And yet in the visions—the sight returned to her constantly each time as if it were fresh and new—she saw that God did not blame us for our sin. The contradiction was terrible for her. It was a "simple thing," an "ordinary thing," and yet she could not resolve it.

Though she could not grasp it, she knew the teaching thoroughly: her revelations taught that not only is sin nothing, not only does it have no substance, but so also, by some mystery, our very sins will be turned into honors. Our sins are somehow needful and by some mysterious way, however shameful, bring honor to God. This seemed to make Jesus like the gardener of her childhood who had turned all the rotten things into delectable fruits. But that alchemy was mysterious to her. How was it done?

"I wept inwardly with all my might," she wrote of her struggle, "searching in God for help." How would she know the answer? "Who is it that shall teach me and tell me what I need to know, if I cannot at this time see it in Thee?"

As she struggled with these issues, the tone of Jesus' voice changed slightly. It was just as loving, just as unfailingly kind, but it was more urgent. When the Lord spoke in her understanding, he seemed, if she dared to admit it, almost exasperated.

"Wouldst thou know thy Lord's meaning?" said that now familiar voice. And then emphatically: "Love was His meaning. Who showed it thee? Love. What showed He thee? Love. Why did He show it thee? For love."

She had to laugh a little at how simple the meaning she sought was and how complex her path to grasping it. But she imagined that she was not alone in struggling to understand that God loves us. Leaning on love, she found herself walking into a deepening trust. As she opened herself up to an honest alignment with the visions, she found herself taking both intellectual and emotional risks that surprised her. She had always been a restless thinker, but now she became a daring one.

ON THE NIGHT OF JUNE 17, 1381, Julian had been meditating on her visions for the better part of a decade when again her city descended into chaos. This time the cause was political. During the reign of King Edward III, England was driven deeply into debt through military campaigns against the French. After his death, under the direction of Richard II and John of Gaunt, in order to raise money for the king's coffers and to continue waging the war, a poll tax was issued, demanding three groats for every member of every household over age fifteen. It was the third such demand in less than five years, and people had soured on the idea. Tension had been building for months. Cattle disease, plague, and drought had left the urban elite, craftsmen, tradesmen, and peasants alike feeling as though they had very little they wanted to offer the king. Rebellion was brewing. In the summer of 1381, the tensions turned bloody.

On June 17, a common dyer named Geoffrey Litster rode into Norwich, claimed ownership of Norwich Castle and declared himself "King of the Common." Litster tried to convince more

reform-minded nobles to support him. Believing the Earl of
Suffolk to be sympathetic, for example, Litster had gone to his
house to ask the earl, William Ufford, to ride with him into Norwich. But by the time Litster arrived, the frightened earl had tak-
en off without finishing his dinner. As rebels ransacked the town,
many died. The rebels set fire to financial records wherever
they could find them, including those found at the priory at
Carrow Abbey.

Henry Despenser defeated the rebels quickly and decisively,
even searching out and arresting those who had taken sanctuary in
churches. He had not been in town when the rebels had arrived,
but once he knew who and where they were, his victory was
swift. The men were arrested, and Despenser, ever their bishop,
took their confessions before having them beheaded. Despenser's
actions were widely praised by the nobility and the king. For the
moment, he was a hero.

Because of her visions, however, Julian saw in the chaos a
question about the nature of sin and God's love. Nothing was
simple: not the king's way, not the peasants' way, not the bishop's
way, not Litster's way. She could not agree with Litster and his
methods, but she knew that the peasants and tradesmen struggled
under heavy taxes. They were bound to their land, but vulnerable
to their lords' whim. They paid most of their harvests to the king
and to their lord, leaving barely enough to feed their families.
Cattle disease and drought stole what little remained. The poorest and most miserable were the peasants who had been thrown
off their land or had lost it. They were compelled to wander
without end, seeking whatever work they could beg or whatever
bread they could steal. Landless peasants were forbidden to work

and, paradoxically, forbidden to roam. They were outcasts. She heard that such people huddled miserably behind buildings on the straithe, hoping to find work unloading at the docks.

Because of their extreme poverty and simmering anger, the peasants were perceived as a threat. The nobility viewed them as one violent hoard, beasts without feeling. Often, lords and peasants did not even speak the same language: the lords spoke French, the language of the court, and the peasants spoke the rough language of the countryside. If common people rose up to protest unjust laws and unjust taxes, they were killed without mercy, dismembered, and parts of their bodies strewn to be eaten by wild animals and their heads hung up on posts as a reminder to others who might dare to defy the social order.

Yet in the vision that had been given to her, as she had asked God for an understanding of sin, Julian had seen an "example." It was unlike much of her visions, more of a story than a symbol, and she had had a difficult time understanding it. But this much she understood: she saw a laborer, a common peasant in a dirty tunic that reminded her of the gardener of her childhood. And she saw his lord. In the showing, the servant went to perform an errand for the lord, and on the way, he fell into a "great slade." He was wounded by his fall and could no longer see his lord. Gradually, accompanied by much meditation, she understood that the servant appeared dirty, wounded, and broken, but in God's eyes he was "assessed as precious." Blind and hurt as he was, he was still God's treasure.

In her visions, Jesus was not a lord like Despenser, meting out justice with the sharp edge of a sword. Instead, when Jesus held a banquet, he took no special place at the table, but "moved throughout his household, filling it full of joy and mirth, in order to endlessly cheer and comfort his dearworthy friends most plainly and most graciously, with marvelous melodies of endless love." Jesus was more bard than lord, interested in our comfort and our delight. He wanted our love more than our submission.

Furthermore, God loved everyone in the same way: herself, Despenser, Litster, the people they had each killed. God reached us in the "lowest part of our need" and did not "disdain to serve us even at the simplest duty." God was as much our servant as we were his. The result of this was the radical understanding at once practical and mystical that we had been "oned together in love."

As these thoughts came clearer to Julian, she knew that she faced a paradox, almost prophetic in its proportions: very few people were ready to hear what she had to say, and yet she could not keep what she was learning to herself. The showings had set fire inside her, and she had to share them. Jesus—her friend, her guide, and her counselor—wished to have his love known more than it was. She had to find a way.

The Seventh Window
WRITING

*"Thou . . . knew not how to preserve it;
but know it now."*
A REVELATION, CHAPTER 70

I N ONE OF JULIAN'S REVELATIONS, Jesus, hanging on the cross, directed her to look into the wound in his side made by the soldier's sword. As she peered into that wound, she glimpsed the whole kingdom of heaven, a "fair, delectable place, and large enough for all mankind that shall be saved to rest in peace and in love." In receiving the visions, a secret door had opened in Julian as well, and through it she saw the kingdom that belonged to all. She was certain that Jesus intended for her to show others what had been shown to her. But how?

As a woman, she was expected to concern herself with private matters, run her household, and devote herself to the church. Preaching and teaching were both unacceptable and impossible. She could not stand on the street corner like a friar and urge people to hear her. True, a very few women like Catherine of

Siena and Bridget of Sweden found ways to influence the people around them, even to advise and counsel popes, but this seemed impossible from her tiny corner of England.

One day, she carried the matter to the friar. She told him of her conviction that she must share what she had seen with others. To both of them, her visions had become like a text that they often spoke of and meditated on. In their studies, one or the other would say, "When Christ showed his precious blood or his wounded side or his dearworthy mother . . . " and they would contemplate together the showings' meanings. But when Julian told him that she must share her visions with others, he was silent a long time.

Finally, he said, "How is it that Catherine of Siena and Bridget of Sweden spread their sweet tellings so far throughout the world? How is it that we come to be speaking of them just now?"

She paused before answering, "By their words. If they had never spoken, we would have heard nothing."

"And how have their words traveled to us that we may hear them, by what means?"

"By parchment. By writing."

"Then," he said, as though the answer had been before him the whole time, "you must write."

The idea seemed preposterous. She stared at him without answering. She carried his words home with her, not daring to laugh at her confessor and yet finding what he had said absurd. Still, on the way home, she passed a parchmenter. Twenty-four leaves for six shillings. Expensive.

She had made a prayer book for her own use. In it, she kept the hours of the Virgin, some of the psalms used for matins, a few prayers and poems that had drawn her attention, and a word or two of Scripture that she had copied from the friar. She was by no means a person of letters. She had learned her alphabet well enough, and now she could read some Latin and English prayers. But she certainly had nothing of the education a person needed to write a book. The idea was ridiculous.

At home, she studied the quill pen that sat next to the book of household accounts. If she were to do this, she would need a large quantity of pens. And the ink! How could she brew enough? Not to mention paper. She opened the account book and stared at the neat rows of figures. She imagined a little column there just for paper. She began to admit to herself that the idea delighted her.

The steps Julian took toward writing were tentative. As she placed her foot on this new ground, she tested it beneath her. When it held steady, she took another step and then another. She put a writing table in the sitting room where they kept the loom and spindle. She affixed calfskin to it and then stared. The hide smelled faintly of the tannery from which it had come. It had a bit of a furry texture. She polished it again with pumice and a goat's tooth and ran her hand over its surface.

She could at least rule the page, she decided. If nothing else, she might copy some psalms onto it. Then it wouldn't be a waste. She carefully measured and ruled, using a chalked string to make fine lines across the page. When that was done, she decanted the ink that had been brewing on the windowsill into a horn and put it into a hole in the writing table. She sharpened the quill with her knife. Now what?

Julian decided to pray. She quieted her mind and her racing heart. She brought herself to a place of rest, the place from which Jesus had so often spoken to her. In the silence that opened inside of her, she heard Jesus say, "You did not know how to preserve what I have shown you, yet I have kept it alive in you. Know it now, know it now that you have a better understanding of it."

She looked again at the parchment in front of her. "Know it now." This paper was not for psalms; it was to preserve the showings, and if it be God's will, to share them.

This became her habit: to pray before, during, and after her writing. The work was holy; it did not belong to her. The ink did not always flow smoothly, and some time passed before Julian was able to press the nib against the paper in just the right way for an even stroke. She saved every scrap of parchment to practice. Brown stains remained on the inside of her index finger, and she took to hiding her hands in her smock. After a writing session, she left the parchment on the writing table to dry and swept up the trimmings from the pen that had fallen on the floor around her. Then she rolled the parchment into a piece of unfinished embroidery. Whenever she saw a good goose quill or a stray nail on the ground, she picked it up and slid it into the pocket of her sleeve. Her eyes, especially in the fall, roved the branches of oak trees for the precious oak gall that with the nail would make ink.

Bit by bit, Julian became the scribe of her own experience. She dared to treat her visions and her meditations on them as a sacred text, demanding to be copied.

In order to frame her words and keep track of what she had written, Julian numbered the visions and numbered the teachings that she had received. Using the visual images that she had received, she tied them carefully in her memory to specific teachings. She memorized the words she had composed so as not to waste any of the precious parchment. The task required far more patience and diligence than Julian had thought herself capable.

Meditating, memorizing, and writing were all demanding, but it was not merely technique that frustrated her. "I cannot show the spiritual visions to you as plainly and fully as I should wish," she wrote as she collided with her own limits and the limits of the written word itself to express what she had seen. She had not known wordlessness like this until she tried to say what was unsayable.

She put down the words that Christ had "formed in her understanding," but she felt that this wasn't enough. Even as Christ said, "Lo, how I love thee," her reader wouldn't know what he meant unless she could somehow put the feeling into it. She decided to try to translate the words of Jesus into other forms, to create the feeling that was in them. "It was as if Jesus had said," she wrote, "'My child, even if thou cannot look upon my divinity, see here how I open my side and how my heart is cloven in two, and how out of it flows the blood and water. This gives me pleasure, and I desire that it do the same for you.'" She used her own translations of Christ's words to show how it felt to encounter the tenderness and openness of God. Though she felt that it still fell short, she layered the visions with her understandings as best she could, believing that this was what Christ required of her.

Often she reached for simple images that she imagined the people around her could grasp. She drew from ordinary life so that the strangeness could inch closer. But sometimes the writing became so frustrating that she squabbled with the very process. "The beauty and vividness of Christ is like nothing but the same," she thought impatiently. And then as she meditated on that statement, she decided, in fact, that is true. It need not be compared to anything. She wrote it down.

MUCH OF WHAT JULIAN HAD LEARNED about the visions came from studies with the friar. But together they discussed how she should treat this learning in the writing. He had taught her far more than any of his other students. He now brought her bits from St. Jerome and St. Augustine; they never tired of pondering together the difficult and intricate writing of St. Paul. But as she meditated on these writings and on her own, she decided not to use them. "Is not Jesus the teacher of all?" she asked.

She had long wanted a life in God, "without intermediaries," and while St. Paul and St. Augustine and St. Jerome and all the good teaching that the friar brought to her attention gave her much knowledge and fed her hungry mind and heart, she wanted to remain true to the purpose that Jesus himself had given her: to write an account of what she had seen. While she was fortunate to receive such teaching, she was strongly convinced that her revelations were for everyone, not only for those who received learning from books. Her visions were for ordinary people, for the "simple."

She and the friar agreed that, if she showed too much of her learning in the writing, there might be two unhappy results. One is that the people she most wanted to speak to, her even Christians, would not see that her writing was intended for them. The other is that it was uncomfortable, even dangerous, for a woman to have the education she now had. Such a powerful tool needed to be kept a secret. The friar was not convinced that she was safe. An educated woman and a visionary was poised on a precipice. If the authorities gained access to her writings, they might conclude that the visions were from the devil. They might see reason to condemn her, to take away her writing materials, to put her in prison, or even to kill her.

Especially in the beginning, as she watched the words—her words—form on paper, she felt ashamed. Who am I to do this? There are so many who love God better. "It should not be said or taken that I am a teacher," she pleaded. "I am a wretched worm, a sinful creature. I am a woman, ignorant, weak, and frail." And then, in her own defense, she wrote in affirmation:

"But should I not tell of the goodness of God that I have seen, that was brought to me by Jesus Christ and that he told me I must share? Let them forget me, the wretch, and behold Jesu the teacher of all."

Writing created exile. However close Julian was physically to her fellow churchmen, however many times a day she encountered them at mass, in her home, and on the street, she had begun to create a life apart. She was alone now in a country where no English woman, certainly no woman that she knew, had ever been before. If it were not for the help of the friar with whom she discussed every detail of the writing, she would not have had the courage to continue. As it was, her courage failed her continually. She worried about her mother, about her neighbors, about the friar, about all who could be harmed because she ventured in this seemingly impossible direction. She worried about the sin and error into which she would no doubt stumble as she began to strive toward a language for the inward teaching. She breathed in and out the words of Jesus, whispered in her own ear, "I keep thee full safely."

When she wrote, she kept images of her neighbors before her. The tanner disfigured by burns, screaming at night in pain, the woman living alone now that all of her ten children were dead, the orphan to whom she brought a piece of the mid loaf so that he might have something soft to put between his teeth. She thought of a prostitute she knew who often sat outside St. Giles dressed in striped clothing with the look of someone so lost, she was no longer searching for home. They all needed to know of the love of God, and while this writing seemed unlikely to reach those who needed it most, it was still an act of love.

She continually rested on the love of God, the one who makes all things well. She was safe because of love. "He who loves thus is safe. And thus will I love, and thus do I love, and thus I am safe. For I stand in for all my even Christians."

The Eighth Window
ENCLOSURE

"He is our clothing which for love enwraps us, holds us,
and all encloses us because of His tender love,
so that he may never leave us."
A REVELATION, CHAPTER 5

HILE JULIAN OFTEN FELT ALONE, she did have one small circle with whom she shared her work and her life. This was the circle of women who met together for matins. For the better part of two decades, this group had shared the common purpose of prayer. These women knew that with the persistence of Julian's questions and the teaching that she was receiving, she needed more space and more time to pray and to write. Every one of them struggled with the dichotomy of Mary and Martha—they wanted more time to devote to spiritual things, but their households demanded much. There were not enough hours in the day for prayer, for the works of mercy, for daily life, for the support and sustenance of their families. They had to train their daughters, arrange households, and make medicines. There were poor to be fed, sick to be tended, dead to be buried. The whole work of the parish rested on their shoulders, just as the work of the household did. The world took the better part of the hours they would devote to prayer. They joked that the number of keys on the rings they wore at their belts was the number they could subtract from the daily offices they were able to perform.

But more than any of them, Julian desired time to meditate on her "ghostly sights" and to write of them. Her writing, as slowly as it progressed, mattered to all of them, and they were eager to see her fully devoted to it.

THE DAY CAME WHEN ONE OF THE WOMEN, after matins, told Julian that she had been thinking: Julian ought to pursue a religious vocation. While she had thought of several possibilities, the role that she thought suited Julian best was anchoress. As an anchoress, Julian could pray and write, but she could also begin to share what she had learned with a wider audience. All of the women knew that was a strong desire for Julian and that she felt constrained in how to pursue it.

The idea answered a question Julian had long been asking herself. She went immediately to the friar for his approval, and he delicately approached the subject: how would she win the bishop's approval? The friar recommended that she prepare a version of her visions for the bishop, perhaps an account of what happened on May 13, 1373, and some of the learning that had followed from it. He urged her not to put in too much. Much of the inward learning was still too delicate to be seen in broad daylight. And she must, he urged, make a great deal of her orthodoxy, her adherence to Holy Church and so on, since the Lollards were beginning to spread heresy and church leaders were wary, particularly of women. Writing itself was enough of a risk, but the friar felt that the bishop would forgive the writing if it was used to express her vocation.

The idea of approaching the bishop with this request was terrifying. Most of the life that had flowed from Julian's visions had been private. People knew that Julian carried with her a great deal of wisdom; they knew they could turn to her for help and hear good counsel. But very few knew of the writing itself. To make that public, to put herself and her life on display for the bishop—that was not something she would have naturally considered. Yet, in prayer, she felt confirmation. So Julian, the friar, and her friends began to work toward enclosure. One of their greatest allies came from a surprising place. One of the women in her circle had a distant connection to the countess of Suffolk, Isabel Ufford. After Isabel's husband's death, Isabel became an anchoress at Campsey Ash. Julian wrote to her, seeking her advice on pursuing her own enclosure, and the countess graciously wrote back. She said that she would personally write to Bishop Despenser since he was a family friend and recommend Julian to him.

For the location of an anchorhold, the women settled on the ancient church of St. Julian's in the neighborhood of Conesford. St. Julian's was located near Conesford Street and was a few minutes' walk from St. Michael's and the friar's home. The rector was old and largely absent; the congregation was small and probably could use some additional income to pay for repair to the thatch. The neighborhood was an odd mix of merchants and tradesman. Butchers, tanners, carpenters, and skinners worked continuously. The church was just steps from the city's largest ports, near a slaughterhouse, and down the hill from Hilldebrond's Hospital where the poorest of the poor were cared for by nuns and "half-sisters."

It was a busy, noisy, smelly location, especially during the day as the boats came into the port. But it was central, inexpensive, and Julian would likely receive a good deal of support. When one of the women expressed concern that it would be too noisy for prayer, Julian countered that living in the midst of industry meant she would be close to her even Christians. Not only that, being so close to the friary meant that the friar could often come to see her.

The single biggest question for establishing Julian in the anchorhold was money. They would have to collect enough to assure the bishop that Julian would never become a problem. Since she would become his responsibility, they needed to assure him that the money to care for her would never come out of his purse. And because the parish was under the protection of Carrow Abbey, Julian would need the blessing of the prioress as well. She would need a small room and a servant to attend her. She would need food, but the women of the parish would likely help to provide it. Once she had established a reputation, it was possible that someone would leave money to her in a will to help pay for necessities of various kinds.

If Julian were to become an anchoress, she would go to live among the graves where she could be dead to the world.

Ironically, however, it also was a central place where she could easily be found by those in the realm of the living who sought her out. Both were important. Being dead to the world would win her the time for prayer and for writing. Being available to her even Christians would help her gain an audience for her visions and the wisdom gleaned from them.

ONCE AN AGREEMENT WAS REACHED with the parish of St. Julian's, the anchorhold was built quickly. It was a flint and stone cottage with a thatched roof and a hazel sedge built in the east part of the churchyard. It had two rooms—one for Julian and one for a servant with a heavy wooden door between the two that could be bolted from the outside. Inside lay a mattress stuffed with bed straw and covered in coarse linen and a wool blanket. The women put a simple table with a removable writing stand and a chair, a bucket for waste, and a bucket for washing. They arranged a small altar with a white cloth covering it, a crucifix, and a picture of Christ's mother and his disciples on either side. They placed on the altar a book of hours to aid in prayer. Julian collected her writing materials and stored them carefully under the table in a wooden box—quills, a pen knife, ink horns, and paper.

In the center of the room was a small stone-lined pit for a fire in which she would burn peat. The women folded a pilch of animal skins and a second woolen blanket in a chest and stored it under the altar. A little porch was attached to the outside wall; there they set up a chair for visitors. On the outside of the porch, they affixed a little box so that people could leave alms for Julian.

The people of St. Julian's parish were eager to have an anchoress living in their midst. They knew nothing of Julian's plans to write, but they watched curiously as the writing desk was moved into the little room, and approvingly as a spindle and embroidery frame were also brought. They stopped by often on their way to and from market to peer through the window, knowing that soon enough a black cloth would be pulled across and they would not see inside.

When it was finished, Julian's room had three windows: one into the servant's room through which she could pass her chamber pot and receive her food, one out onto the porch to receive visitors, and a cross-shaped window in the direction of the church. Her space was fresh and cheerful, if simple. Julian found it delightful, imagining that it contained exactly the paradoxical freedom for which she had searched.

A woman named Alice agreed to work as Julian's maid. She, too, longed for the contemplative life, but was still unsure of her calling. Together they would serve the people of the community, with Alice caring for the outside world and Julian for the interior lives of the people.

At last everything was ready: the bishop, urged by the countess, had agreed to their plan, the anchorhold was complete, and a date was set for the enclosure ceremony.

ON THE AUTUMN NIGHT BEFORE HER ENCLOSURE, Julian knelt in her mother's house before the window. The night air was sharp; the incessant wind tossed the beech and alder, sending patterns of shifting leaves across the floor. She had spent hours and hours kneeling here. Just exactly here was where the true form of prayer had taken shape in her and she in it. Her gray woolen kirtle pulled a little against her knees. Tomorrow she would take on the black robe of an anchoress.

When she thought of what she would miss about her life outside the anchorhold, she thought of the parish in which she had grown up. The people of the parish had guided her through her childhood, through the deaths of her children and now the death of her mother, through her preparations for the anchorage. She thought about how she would never again light a candle at her favorite altar. She would never again sample Mother Katherine's ale in the parish hall or decorate for a dance. She would never again slip along still quiet streets on her way to meet her friends for matins. She would miss the way that one woman in their group would begin by singing the words, "O Lord, open my lips," and the others would answer, "And my mouth shall shew forth thy praise" as they stood together, arms uplifted.

BUT THE TRUTH WAS that her separation from her community was already long begun. The inward teaching needed more time to work on her. She remembered a moment when the idea of the anchorhold became real to her. She had been praying fervently for one of her friends who was facing a time of trial. She asked God what would happen to her friend and begged God to remove the pain from her. But as she prayed, she began to see her error. She should not pray for any one person or any one circumstance. Instead, God was the ground of her prayer. She must root and dwell in him, so that she could tell all of his mercy and grace. If she became an anchoress, she could speak to all and stand in for all. Tomorrow, she would make a covenant with the community of St. Julian's to stay by them until her death, offering them this ground of her prayer.

She wanted to stay on her knees until the first light of morning when her friends came. She wanted to see that slow gray light steal once again across just exactly this patch of sky and inch upward. She wanted to hear the sweet twittering in the trees that signaled dawn. As at the time of her illness, a procession would come for her, but this time, it would lead her to a different kind of death, a death to celebrate. She fell asleep just as the first crow cackled in the winter sky, and she awakened when her friends arrived to take her to St. Julian's.

THE PROCESSION BEGAN AT JULIAN'S HOUSE, and as it moved along Conesford Street, more and more people gathered behind until there was a large crowd. Together they turned up the alley and entered the church. People from her parish joined people from St. Julian's; the friar and her friends encircled her.

Inside the church, Bishop Despenser stood partially concealed behind the rood screen while he put on his rich vestments and chanted, *"Confiteor Deo omnipotenti et vobis, fratres, quia peccavi nimis. . . . "*

As the psalms were intoned, Julian went to the west part of the church and lay flat against the ground, surrounded by all the women present. She lay against the cold stones of the floor while the bishop, in a crowd of priests, approached with cross, holy water, and smoky puff of the thurible. He swung it over her, chanting, *"Veni Sancti Spiritus."* Another priest sprinkled her with water, the soft drips sensible through her linen shift. She shivered.

They led her to the center altar of the church where she again lay down. "Let her think," the bishop said aloud, "that she is convicted of her sins and committed to solitary confinement as to a prison, and that on account of her own weakness she is unworthy of the fellowship of mankind."

Raised to her feet, the women gave her two candles, one for each hand. A priest read in a solemn voice, "Come, my people, enter thou into thy chambers, and shut thy doors about thee: hide thyself as it were for a little moment, until the indignation be overpast."

The friar, as her confessor, read from the Gospels in Latin, the story of Mary and Martha. Julian knew the story well. Jesus praised Mary for taking the quieter part, for relinquishing, at least for a moment, a woman's unending work in the world and settling herself at Jesus' feet, as she was now doing.

After professing her faith in Holy Church and her acceptance of the bishop's authority, she knelt on the church's stone floor and said three times, "Receive me, O Lord, according to Thy word." Once she said those words, a heavy black robe was placed over her linen shift and a black veil arranged over her hair.

The bishop led the procession outside, where the anchorhold stood waiting like a tiny child crouched in the churchyard. Walking behind him, she could study this man who had been the center of so much gossip. She could tell by his gait that he was still proud, every bit the nobleman, but his shoulders were hunched slightly, and if she looked carefully, he seemed to walk favoring his right side, as if in pain. The bishop was a man of her same age, but he looked quite youthful. She could see just a trace of his failed crusade against Pope Clement VII that had brought him home in defeat and debt. The church had taken away his "temporalities," his income, in order to pay back the debt, a humiliating loss. Whereas he had often wandered far from the diocese, these days he stayed closer to home. He clearly loved ceremonies, like this one, where draped in gold and ermine, he carried the scepter.

Outside the door of the anchorhold, the choir continued to sing, *"Veni Sancti Spiritus."* Then the choir sang,

> O key of David and scepter of Israel,
> what you open no one can close again;
> what you close no one can open.
> O come to lead the captive from prison;
> free those who sit in darkness and in the shadow of death.

The bishop entered the anchorhold first with the rector and the parish clerk. They incensed the room, sprinkling it with holy water and chanting prayers of blessing. When they were finished, the bishop stepped back through the door into the damp air and said without looking at Julian, "He who wishes to enter, let him enter."

The bishop returned inside with Julian following and all the people crowded behind, spilling into the yard. The priest began the office of the dead. As the priest and congregants said the office, they added Julian's name, as she now descended into the dead and left her place among the living. Dust was scattered at her door and the bishop intoned, "From dust you were created, to dust you shall return."

Then the whole crowd turned, and when they had all filed out, the parish clerk bolted the door. Julian was alone. The room breathed its newness—the white plaster of the walls, the freshly installed beams of the ceiling, the new reeds on the floor. The room smelled of sweet bay. She might have wept for all that had been done for her to bring her here to this glorious silence. Though the noise of the crowd and the smell of the thurible still lingered, the silence itself was incense.

The Ninth Window
SWEET SPIRITUAL SIGHTS

"And thus shall we, by his sweet grace,
in our own meek continual prayer,
come into him now in this life by many secret
touchings
of sweet spiritual sights and feelings,
measured out to us as our simplicity may bear.

And then we shall come into our Lord, clearly
knowing and God fully having, and we shall all
be endlessly hidden in God, truly seeing and
wholly feeling, and hearing him spiritually and
delectably smelling and sweetly tasting him."
A REVELATION, CHAPTER 43

I N MARCH OF 1393, a few years after Julian's enclosure, the first bequest came: Roger Reed, the rector at a Norwich church, St. Coslany, left her two shillings. His offering provided a small income so that she could send Alice to the parchmenter for paper or she could buy a few eggs on a feast day. While large gifts did not come, small ones came every day. Women brought baskets of plums or picked up an extra loaf of bread for her when they stopped by the community oven. They brought her nuts and fruit from their trees or dropped pennies in her alms box. During canning time, they brought jam. The women of the church knew that it was their duty to care for her, and her duty to pray for them, so they were careful to provide her with what she needed. It was a relationship, not exactly of obligation, but of intricate mutual support. They believed that Julian's prayer provided a blanket for them as solid, as necessary, as tangible as their own woolen weavings that hung on her walls to keep her warm.

The leadership at St. Julian's changed hands frequently. When the old rector died, the new one that was appointed never came, so the people attended mass at St. Stephen's up the street. The appointed rector of St. Julian's quickly traded his post for another, and a different man was appointed. This meant that Julian, as her months in the anchorhold turned into years, was a more stable presence for the people of the parish than their rector. They turned to her for counsel, and while she could not absolve them, she could draw them deeper into a life of prayer and trust.

Now that she was enclosed, she no longer went to St. Michael's at the friary, but the old friar came to her. He entered the porch after terce, his presence as gentle and difficult to detect as ever. She listened closely for him from behind the black curtain, but not until he pulled a reeded chair close to the anteroom window did she hear him. Alice had placed a basket of wild rose hips there and the smell filled the small space like a tiny mystery. The day would be warm, but the porch had a lingering morning coolness.

"Benedicite," Julian said from behind the curtain.

"Dominus te benedicat," he answered.

Then he said, "How fares thee, child? I've brought something wonderful." Through the curtain, she could imagine the twinkle in his eyes. She knew that it took him longer these days to walk up the street from the friary. His hands trembled a bit as he pulled a book from his robe and passed it through the window so that Julian could hold it. The book's binding was white leather, yellowing at the creases. Its pages were smooth, almost silky, and the monk's writing was precise. The capitals were drawn with a bit of red and a bit of blue ink.

"It's beautiful, Father," she said passing the book back through the black curtain.

"This is Father Augustine, blessed be he," the friar said, clearing his throat. *"Dei Civitas.* The City of God. The part I want to read today is about the relationship between God and the soul." He began to read, first in Latin and then translating.

"Father Augustine teaches that there are two cities: one of God and one of man. One based on love and one on death. Man is of both cities and dwells in both at once. Here he says that God made man in his own image. He created for him a soul endowed with reason and intelligence so that he might surpass all the creatures of earth and sea, those not so gifted. When God had formed man from the dust of the earth, he breathed on him, imparting the soul."

Julian imagined the good and courteous Lord breathing into the mouth of the lifeless man. It was an image of stark tenderness, intimacy, goodness. She startled herself by saying, "Do God and the soul share the same nature by sharing this breath?"

As always, the friar was calm and careful with his words. This conversation was now twenty years old, and it contained long pauses. The friar was an old man. On the space on his scalp cleared for his tonsure were liver spots. That beloved preaching voice had worn thin.

"What would it be to share the same nature?" he asked. She looked down at her knitting—the way that one tiny piece of thread linked itself to another so that they became inextricable. To rend one would destroy the whole. "Mankind's dearworthy soul was preciously knit to him in the creation," she said, "and this knot is delicate and so powerful that it is oned into God." She paused. "In this, it is made endlessly holy."

Alice brought them a meal of ale and furmity, and they ate together, one on each side of the curtain. He brought her news of her friends and of St. Michael's. Then he blessed her, wished her well in her prayers, and promised to return as soon as he was able. She ardently wished that she could reach through the curtain and kiss his cheek before he left. Instead she reached her hand through the curtain, and his warm, gentle, rough hand grasped it.

LATER, IN HER PRAYERS, Julian saw St. Augustine's two cities. One was ruled by her good lord, a lord who dined and laughed, who so loved the people of his city that he did not even take his royal throne. He roamed among his guests, laughing when they laughed, adding mirth and joy everywhere he went. She had seen something like this in her visions, although she hadn't known if it was a castle or a kingdom or a city. She only knew that this beautiful place was inside of her and that Jesus had declared it his eternal dwelling.

The other city was dominated by a cruel and oppressive lord. People shrank in fear; the streets were empty as they had been during the worst days of the pestilence. The lord was not just. He meted out punishment without care. He ruled rashly by wrath. As the people suffered, he laughed.

In her prayers, as so often happened, two motions occurred at once. In one motion, she saw the city of death enclosed in love, wrapped like a crying child in swaddling rags. In the other, she saw the gates of the city of love opened wide. People streamed in and out. They roamed freely in endless bliss and back into the city of the Lord. Then she saw the city of God in her, spread out like a shining jewel. There in it, wrapped and enclosed by her own flesh, was Jesus himself. "We are so oned," said Jesus to her, "that I am never out of you and you are never out of me."

Every showing was full of secrets, and she had begun to detect a pattern in how the unfolding of secrets took place. She would often see the vision just as it had been the first time; she would feel the same emotions and see the same sights. But then the showing would expand. New meanings would be added on top of the old. The friar's teaching combined with her own meditations to allow her to see something entirely new. And then God would show her the entire revelation again, so that she could incorporate this new understanding into the whole.

She often saw Jesus suffering on the cross, bleeding profusely as he had that day so many years ago when she feared that his blood would soak the bed where she lay. When she remembered fearing that his blood would soak the bed, she thought of the blood of childbirth. She then saw that the suffering of Christ on the cross was not like the suffering of the pestilence or other horrors she had known. It was not an empty black hole of despair. Instead it was the suffering of giving birth. He carried us within himself in love, and labored until full term so that he could suffer the sharpest throes and the hardest pains. But when he had finished, and given birth to bliss, he still was not satisfied. He said, "If I could suffer more, I would suffer more."

"Is there any pain in hell like this?" she asked him.

"Hell is a different pain," he answered. "For there is despair." Jesus' pain was the pain of compassion, the pain of a mother in labor. She saw that Jesus was our mother, giving birth to us on the cross. She saw that we are endlessly born and yet we never come out of God.

IN THE ANCHORHOLD, JULIAN COUNTED the years since the first vision. Twenty years, short three months, February 1393. The anchorage was cold in February, and stoking the fire only helped so much. She and Alice counted the stacked peat dwindling in the anteroom, and then meted it out more carefully. It was still dark in the anchorhold a good part of the day, and so Julian did not take out her writing desk as much as she would like. But on a bitter February day, with a sleet-like rain falling, she returned to that strange and wonderful parable of the lord and the servant. Her visions were often renewed by "lighteninges and touchinges." The Lord often brought more sight at the most surprising times, leaving her always to wonder. Many times she had pondered what the parable meant, but she made little progress. In her inward teaching, she was now instructed to go over the parable slowly and take in each detail. She paid attention to the color of the servant's cloak and the color of the lord's; she paid attention to the color of the sky and of the throne on which the Lord sat. She studied her vision as if studying a painting in church.

Gradually, she saw something that took her breath away. She had long understood that the lord did not blame the servant for falling into the slade and being wounded. She understood that the lord loved the servant as before. But today, she saw something new: the servant was Adam, but the servant was also Christ. There was only one fall, and Christ and Adam took this fall together. Adam was Christ and Christ was Adam. Perhaps this radical understanding of the parable had prevented her from accepting it for so long. God's love for us was exactly the same as God's love for Christ. No, even more than that. We were Christ. Christ was us. Christ was our mother, our lover, and our brother, and even ourselves—bound to us by as many kinds of love as exist.

With this understanding, and with the lengthening of the days, she began to write now more freely than she had ever thought possible. She no longer protested to the voice inside her that she was the wrong person for this work. Shame and fear took their leave.

This inner freedom had not come because the world outside validated and understood her. It had not come from accolades from the bishop for the great work of her anchorage. In fact, the very experience of inner freedom was contradicted by what she heard and knew of the world outside. The friar told her that the archbishop of Canterbury had announced he would severely punish women for teaching, and that no one should write of religious matters in English. She heard siren calls of heresy on every side, though not yet directed at her. Attention focused on a group of people called Lollards. These people kept Bibles in English in their homes and rejected contemplation and prayer. They ate meat on Fridays. Some Lollards asserted that women might be more suitable ministers of the sacrament than men. In 1397, a group of bishops including Henry Despenser requested the right to kill Lollards, and they began searching people's homes for English Bibles. The first Lollards—men, women, and children—were burned in Norwich in 1401 near Bishop's Gate at a place called Lollard's Pit.

Julian shuddered to think of what she had written, "Holy Church shall be shaken in sorrow and anguish and tribulation in this world, as men shake a cloth in the wind." Jesus' words, formed in her understanding, were even more fierce, and she had written those as well, "I shall totally shatter you because of your vain affections and your vicious pride and after that I shall gather you together and make you humble and gentle, pure and holy, by oneing you to myself." The scandal raged in places far and near from her small house in St. Julian's yard, and she knew that her words would not be well received by those in power. As the fears grew in all corners, she heard rumors. She'd heard of an anchoress, one Matilda of St. Peter's Leicester, who had been dragged from her cell to account for some sayings that were too learned. She had been sent to a convent to learn a simpler faith.

Yet Jesus had said to Julian, "I keep thee full safely." He had said this "with more love and steadiness and spiritual protection than I know how or am able to tell." She assumed that he meant that her soul was protected, that she did not need to fear sin and error as she had when she first dipped her pen into ink in an act of frightening permanence. But he seemed also to mean that the anchorage could be for her a place of peace and safety.

Perhaps she had finally grasped what long eluded her: that sin truly was nothing. Even doubtful dread, that cold wind of uncertainty that had so often blown over her, was no longer hateful to her. Instead she saw that it was a way of turning her heart to God. The bitterness of doubt could become the sweetness of gentle love by God's grace. She was indeed safe from every bellow of the devil, every terrible wind that blew.

The Tenth Window
ANCHORESS

*"God is being
and wants us to sit, dwell and ground
ourself in this knowledge
while at the same time realizing
that we are noble, excellent,
assessed as precious and valuable
and have been given creation
for our enjoyment
because we are loved."*
A REVELATION, CHAPTER 42
(BRENDAN DOYLE'S TRANSLATION)

T HE YEARS IN THE ANCHORHOLD unfolded
slowly, and Julian noticed from the stiffness in her
joints when she got up in the morning and the way
that cold settled on her that she was growing old. On
the table in front of her lay a hazelnut. It was last fall's hazelnut,
and it had been sitting in her room in a reed basket for several
months, awaiting shelling. The hazelnut was a rich, soft copper.

Her revelation was no longer—had not been for years—a moment in time, but had come to encompass all time. The writing was a revelation; the meditating was a revelation; the people who came to see her at the anchorage: they were revelations. The frontier for which the younger Julian longed, that place beyond the church, beyond the already known boundaries of space and time, she had now walked for many years. And she hadn't reached its end. Each moment of discovered truth opened up yet another unexpected horizon, and she now knew that beyond this moment was one still more immense, still greater, and more surprising. Her small room, this small table, this tiny hazelnut—they all contained vast universes of revelation. From one "showing" came hundreds of hours of thought, prayer, hope, and love. She saw something. She wrote it down. Everything was still more "ghostly and more sweetly than I can or may tell it." Truth was not a moment. Not something that could be held in the palm of one's hand, like a hazelnut. Truth was a vast country that must be entered, explored, experienced, and finally loved. Somehow, right here, in these earthen walls, the entire landscape of God spread out in front of her. A free enclosure.

She lived in the anchorage accompanied by peace. In the mornings, waking before the Angelus bell, she crossed herself and said out loud, "In the name of the Father and the Son and the Holy Ghost." Kneeling on the uneven warp of her woolen blanket, she raised her arms upward and said, "Come, O Holy Spirit, come." She relieved herself in a chamber pot and set the pot near the door. After pulling her black robe over her head and securing it with a belt around her waist, she sprinkled herself with holy water and knelt at her altar for the first meditation of the day.

An anchoress was instructed to live slowly—to make each act a deliberate one. The raising of her arms in her first prayers, the movement to her knees, the recitation of the first psalms: "O Lord, open thou my lips, and my mouth shall shew forth thy praise"—were all done in slow, prayerful motion.

After prayer she washed with water from the leather-lined bucket and again knelt at her altar. Seven times a day, she paused like this, keeping the liturgy of the hours. All day long, she heard the flow of prayers at the altars of St. Julian's, high mass and low masses, spreading out like a constantly woven and then unraveled and rewoven tapestry. She walked over in the early morning to attend the first mass of the day, slipping out through the wooden door, feeling the grass beneath her feet and breathing deeply the air that smelled a bit like fish and a bit like lime and a bit sour, like animal blood. She smelled rain, must and damp, and peat smoke. She saw that the rector's vegetable garden was overrun with the thick leaves of kale.

She stood by the leper's squint and peered in as the priest lifted the bread. In the churchyard at her feet, she saw love-lies-a-bleeding and lady's mantle, shepherd's purse, currant berries, and lemon balm. She wondered if Sarah, the servant who had replaced Alice, might want to dry some black currant leaves for tea before they turned bitter. She ought to tell her that there used to be some sweet cicely that grew on the side of St. Michael's.

After mass came Julian's meal. In the Easter season, she had two meals a day. In the other seasons, just one. Sarah put them through her window—a little ale, barley broth, or porridge with nuts, dried herring, cocket bread with butter, a boiled parsnip with parsley and salt. In the evenings, Sarah brought her a cup of sage tea. If a soft rain was falling, she could hear robins making a fuss as they picked at the grass. A group of them made a nest in the cross-shaped window of her house every summer, and in the churchyard, she could hear the sound of tiny woodpeckers searching for insects in the trees. When the doves cooed, their voices echoed eerily through the room.

On Sundays, parishioners processed through the churchyard, sprinkling holy water on the graves. They called out to her as they came by. "Good day, Mother Julian. Blessings on you!" On St. Peter's Day they brought her bread, beer, and cheese and sang outside her door. Next to the anchorhold was a carpenter's workshop, on the other side a fuller's shop for making cloth. A calvesyard was across the way on Ber Street so that the breeze often smelled sickly sweet and sour, and the squeal of dying animals was a frequent counterpoint to prayer. St. Julian's was a place where the sounds and smells of daily life could ever enter. Hammers, carts, boatmen shouting from the pier, the carpenter calling to his apprentice—all of life was never far from Julian's window.

She set up her writing in the early afternoon when the light was good, but more and more her attention was focused on the time after nones when the people came to her window for advice and counsel. She pulled a chair next to the window and took up her knitting so that she could keep her hands busy while she listened. And mostly that was what she did: listen.

They brought with them every kind of dilemma and sorrow—illness, death, heartache, and fear. Her fame as a good listener and kind counselor spread. Anchoresses were already revered for maintaining a deep well of prayer from which the people could draw. But Julian became more than that. She had insight, and she spoke carefully. Other anchorites and hermits began to send people to her, where they could expect a gracious reception. In this way, quietly, Julian became a significant presence, well known among those who would "learn to love God better."

Her expertise became discernment. She knew the way that the Holy Spirit spoke through a "rest in soul and a quietness in conscience." People came to her asking to know whether messages came from God or the devil. Every day she saw evidence that "love and fear are brothers," and she tried to help people make their way between them. Sometimes she felt she had nothing to say but, "This life is a muddle, I know it myself. A mix of well and of woe. Although we feel miseries, disputes, and strifes in ourselves, yet we are all mercifully enwrapped in the mildness of God and in His humility, in His kindliness, and in His gentleness."

Sometimes the people at her window begged her to tell them if some person that they loved would be saved. They lived in horror of the tortures of purgatory and the hopelessness of hell. When they saw purgatory in their visions, they saw their loved ones or themselves pricked by thousands of needles or fed with toads. Julian could not always offer them the succor they wanted. She herself had received no visions of hell or of purgatory. "God is all love," she offered. "He is all mercy and all grace. There is no wrath in God." She often felt that she was speaking to the black curtain alone and that her words floated no farther than an inch from her mouth. They wanted her to tell them that she had seen this or that loved one saved from the jaws of hell by the flight of angels or that Mary had come to her and personally whispered the name of the one who would be saved. Julian did not see these kinds of visions, and she could only tell them honestly that she saw no wrath in God. She felt their disappointment, but she hoped that something of God's love might echo for them, long into the future.

People's view of God often seemed to her lacking in one crucial area: love. The people who came to her window believed that God was almighty; he could do with them whatever he liked. They believed that God knew all things, especially that he was able to peer into their weak and frail hearts. But where most people failed—and she had seen this even in those who had the most stature in the church—was in believing that God was all love, that God loved them enough to want to make all things well. Ignorance of love—that was a miserable failing.

So Julian repeated daily to the people who came to her window, "Our courteous Lord loves us." She paused. If she felt she could go on, she added, "I am convinced if God does not appear to give us what we most truly ask, it is because we are to await a better time or more grace or a better gift.

"God wants us to root ourselves in His being, in His love. All gifts that we long for come from that."

She cautioned them not to imagine that we could sway God into action on our behalf by the right combination of prayers and holy living. "We do not move God to love us by praying. God is ever the same in love." Again she waited, giving the person at her window time to ponder this, just as Christ so thoughtfully paused in his teaching of her.

She relied on small, prudent, and subtle conversations. She carefully shaped her words to each individual, and yet the message was always the same: whatever your dilemma, the answer you are seeking is found in love. She taught prayer and trust—two things that people found impossible. And when they were not ready for either of these, she told them of her own experience and of the day that Jesus said to her, "You will not be overcome." "Notice," she said, "he did not say you will not be tempested. He did not say you will not be travailed. He did not say you will not be disquieted. But he did say, 'You will not be overcome.'"

WHILE HUNDREDS OF PEOPLE stopped by Julian's window in the almost thirty years that she lived in the anchorage, history records only one: Margery Kempe. Margery came to Julian because she had heard the anchoress knew whether visions contained deceit. She herself had experienced many visions, but she was not sure how to understand them. Margery sought advice from every spiritual teacher she could find. To each one, she asked if the teacher could detect any deceit in her revelations. When she came to Julian's window, she brought the same question she had asked Julian's neighbor at the Carmelite monastery at Fishergate, William Southfield, and same question for which she had just consulted Richard Caister at St. Stephen's.

At Julian's window, she again told her story, pouring out its details, wishing that she could see the face of the woman behind the black curtain. From the other side of the curtain came silence.

When at last Margery paused in her telling, Julian remained quiet for a time. Then she said, "Thanks be to God, Sister. The discerning of spirits is not so difficult as you imagine. The test is charity. The Holy Ghost would never counsel us against charity, for he is all love and to do so would be against his very nature."

The next day, Margery returned again. This time, Julian put her finger directly, but gently on Margery's greatest difficulty.

"The Holy Ghost makes a soul to be stable and steadfast. You see how we can be shaken, moved about like a cloth in the wind. And doubting moves us like a flood moves to the sea. But God comes with compassion, and his love for us is unending. We discover a rest in the soul. We need not search far away to discover this. We can learn at our Mother's breast, in our own souls."

When Margery left, Julian's head ached. She could feel the burden of each person who had come as if they had each handed her a stone to carry in her heart. She understood why the Holy Ghost had counseled her not to pray for anyone in particular, but only for the well-being of all. Praying and worrying for each in particular could become a painful burden if she let it.

Julian lit the candles for compline. Before bed, she said the Paternoster, the Ave Maria, and the Nunc Dimittis. She rubbed hazel oil on her heels and listened to the soft thud of the rain on the thatch. She lay down, looked up at the diamond-shaped crisscross of the sedge, and asked again to love God better.

All shall be well, but the work of love was always ongoing.

A DEED HONORABLE, MARVELOUS, AND PLENTEOUS

"Our Lord God showed me that a deed shall be done and He Himself shall do it; and it shall be honorable and marvelous and plenteous, and through me it shall be done, and He Himself shall do it."
A REVELATION, CHAPTER 36

O N THE VERY LAST SUNDAY OF THE CHURCH YEAR, before the season of Advent marked a new beginning, the priest read from the Letter of Paul to the Philippians. "He that began in you a good work shall perform it until the day of Jesus Christ." It was a phrase on which Julian had meditated many times. She had taken it to live inside her. She wondered about the "work" and what of it was "good." She wondered about what it would mean to have it finally "performed" like that Great Deed on the day when, at last, all shall be well.

Her own book of visions, as she saw it, was also not yet performed. It was a circle within a circle within a circle. Even though unfinished and imperfect, she declared it done. She gave the pages a final wash of egg white to preserve the ink. She bound it herself, stitching the pages together and securing them between two pieces of wood. She ordered a piece of soft leather from the tanner, and she covered the wood and secured the leather with wheat paste. Then she held it in her now wrinkled hands for a long time. She hoped that it would evoke from its readers a response of love. God's love was a cycle of giving that had no beginning and never ended. God never started to love us, but loved us before we existed and brought us into being. And thus God's love never ended: not in death and in judgment, not in sin and pain. It was the very ground of our existence.

God had shown her that the landscape of love was an endless expanse, and yet was contained, just as all visions were contained in the first. Each flowed out of and into another. Understanding began in the showings, continued through the inward learning and outward into living. The riches of Christ's gifts were never fully explored and never finally understood. The soul in Christ and Christ in the soul were endlessly oned and endlessly oneing.

She could not see forward to who might read this work. It was fragile, and it would become dust. Many of the people to whom she had spoken her word of love could not read, and so though her book was meant for her even Christians, she could only hope that someone would read it to them. But in her soul was whispered a secret: God was doing a great work. This tiny work of hers was a part of a great work of God's, and somehow, he would use it. This is the highest joy that her soul understood: that God himself would do it! Her sin and her failings could not impede God's work. Her impatience, her sloth, her weariness could not hinder his goodness. The work was not hers, but God's, and he would see it to completion. In God's life, love, and light, she could put the strength and outcome of the revelation, and then let it be.

After long contemplation, she decided to pass the book out the window and hope that it found friends. She entrusted the book to a young nun at Carrow Abbey, a woman who came to see her often. This nun copied it and sent it to the nuns at the new abbey dedicated to St. Bridget, Syon Abbey near London. In this way, hand to hand, the book found its way into libraries.

ONE DAY, EARLY IN 1417, NEWS of Countess Isabel Ufford's death arrived at Julian's window. The countess left Julian the sum of twenty shillings, and Julian smiled at the thought of her longtime correspondent remembering her. Isabel's niece, Emma, was interested in becoming an anchoress, but was anxious about what her father might say. The three women had exchanged many letters on the subject. Emma, a frail girl of striking intelligence, saw the anchorage as a place where she could pursue an education in peace. But her father, a nobleman whose family had a long history in Norfolk, hesitated to make the necessary arrangements.

Julian herself knew that death was very near. She had chosen the anchorage as a first death and burial. Through it she had been able to become an anonymous person of prayer. But in this next death, she could at last "cleave to the one Goodness" and pass finally into the light. She imagined herself buried in this very ground on which she had walked for so many years. She imagined her bones scooped up with others and moved into the bone house where they would disintegrate. She imagined the long-awaited clarity of sight, when at last her light would be full and complete.

Meanwhile, Julian continued to pray. She walked in the church-yard to mass, and then returned to her solitude with the door firmly closed and curtain drawn. She had learned to detect in everything—the calendula growing bright orange in the hedge-row, the tiny gooseberries, the garlic mustard in her porridge—the presence of God. It was a quality of listening, a way of paying attention. In this way, life had begun and would end in love.

ONE DAY, AS THE CEASELESS NORFOLK WIND blew strong across the river tossing the branches of the oaks in the churchyard at St. Julian's, Sarah failed to hear any stirrings or the murmur of morning prayers in the other room, and when she brought the meal after terce and spoke out a greeting, Julian did not answer. The old anchoress had slipped quietly into the "endless day."

Word of Julian's death spread rapidly through the neighborhood. People brought small gifts to put outside her window and stood in quiet groups in the churchyard. Sarah and the rector made arrangements for her burial, and in the tradition of anchorites, her grave was unmarked. For a time, the neighborhood people continued to leave small offerings on the mound of freshly overturned earth under which her body lay. The seasons changed, snow fell, grass grew, ivy crept over the soil, and the last traces of Julian's physical being disappeared.

The rector made arrangements for another anchorite to move into her little cell, and one after another, for a hundred years, Julian's tradition of prayer, solitude, and counsel continued from that very same place. The names of the other anchorites who came to live there were Julian, Agnes, and Elizabeth. They carried forward Julian's example of a simple life rooted in God's love.

BUT THE DEED THAT JULIAN HAD ENVISIONED—the one that God had told her would be done through her—was, just as she had said, "not yet performed." Her book, the first copy carefully made by her own hands, had gone out from her window and into the world. Copies of it were then made by others who longed to "love God better." One version was even included in an anthology of contemporary writings near the time of her death. Her strikingly personal, intimate, and womanly voice interrupts and disrupts the pedagogical tones of other more church-sanctioned writers. Another version (selections from the longer text) guides nuns practicing enclosure at the end of the fifteenth century. Her book finds its way to the shelves of libraries in monasteries, convents, and "chapter houses" throughout England. Copies were burned in the dissolution, and copies of *A Revelation of Love* accompanied exiled Catholics across the English Channel to France.

All along the way, the words, "All shall be well, all shall be well, all manner of all things shall be well," traveled with Julian's book, speaking differently to each generation and to each reader. Some found in her writings consolation; some found challenge; some found a "fanatik" and "blasphemous nonsense." Some stumbled onto Julian like finding a long-lost friend.

Until our own day, when Julian's words are ubiquitous: in anthologies and devotional guides, collections of prayers, and even books about gardening. Her words have traveled far to meet us, planting tiny seeds of both light and hope as they go.

When we encounter Julian's words now, we join a great crowd of her even Christians, each of us uniquely challenged to grapple with the radical possibility that "faith is nothing else but a right understanding and trust of our being, that we are in God and God, whom we do not see, is in us." Faith, in other words, might be nothing else than letting God's great work be done, through Julian, in us.

WE HAVE NO RECORD of anyone reading Julian's words in her own lifetime. The first record of a reader comes from the seventeenth century at a place in France called Cambrai. There, in 1623, a Benedictine monk named Augustine Baker arrived at a house of English-speaking Benedictine nuns. The nuns had asked for help with contemplative prayer, and Baker was an expert. He brought with him, among many manuscripts, a copy of Julian's book.

Baker was an iconoclast; he counseled the women to seek their own way in prayer and not to rely too heavily on any authority. This and many of his other teachings were controversial. One of the nuns credited Baker on her deathbed with the fact that she was comfortable passing into the next life without the aid of a priest or any intermediary.

Two of the four remaining manuscripts of *A Revelation of Love* come from these nuns and this time period. The older of the two is a large, clumsy book that appears to have been made swiftly. The handwriting is a difficult scrawl. Gone are the carefully formed letters of the monastic tradition. The ink bleeds from one page to the next. It is almost as if the nun who copied it did not intend for anyone else to read it, but made it for her own use, maybe to be copied more carefully later. But here is the full text—every word of what remains of Julian's legacy.

At the very end of the manuscript lies a note from a scribe, perhaps not the Cambrai nun, but from a previous generation of scribes. It hovers at the end of Julian's manuscript, a long and nervous commentary on the text.

> I pray almighty God that this Book does not come into the hands of anyone except those who will be his faithful lovers, and those that will submit themselves to the faith of the Church and obey the wholesome understanding and teaching of the Men who are of virtuous life, sadage, and profound learning: for the Revelation is high Divinity and high wisdom, wherefore it cannot survive with him that is slave to sin and to the Devil. And beware that thou not accept one thing after thine own inclination and liking and leave another for it is the condition of a heretic. But accept each thing with the other and truly understand that all is in agreement with Holy Scripture and grounded in the same, and that Jesus our very love, light, and truth shall shew this wisdom to all clean souls that with meekness ask with perseverance of him. And thou to whom the Book shall come thank highly and heartily our Savior Christ Jesus, that he made these shewings and Revelations for thee and to thee

of his endless love, mercy, and goodness for our
safe guide and conduct to everlasting bliss, which
Jesu might grant us. Amen.

The person who wrote this note unquestionably feared that
Julian's words could disrupt the foundations of the church or
unravel the human heart. This "colophon" is meant as protection
both from and for Julian's words as they venture out into a cruel and
misunderstanding world. By opening ourselves to love, the writer
fears, we risk wandering in the territory of heretics. While Julian
wrote to all her even Christians, this scribe anxiously confined
Julian's words only to those with already proper inclinations.

But there is another manuscript that comes from this same
group of nuns. This manuscript is smaller. The carefully made
script has a modern personality and lightness about it. In the
margins, in the same handwriting as the text, the scribe left
notes: "Wonderful!" and, "How we should make petition to our
Ld God."

At the end of the manuscript, the nun who scribed this
manuscript repeated the admonition of the previous one. She
copied the warning that the revelation "cannot survive" one who
is slave to sin. She copied the prayer that the book not lead the
reader astray. But then she left a small space. Perhaps that space
was filled with a silence like Julian's silence, as if the scribe paused
to draw on that deep well of prayer Julian had also tapped. I
imagine her putting the quill back on the tray for a moment and
rising from her chair. She noticed a disquiet inside her created by
the words of admonition and warning that she had just written. She
went to stand by the window of the library and looked through

the diamond-shaped glass of the room. Outside, a Paris mist had almost swallowed the gardens.

Julian's words had stirred her. She had felt, reaching toward her, a woman whose heart had been broken and then expanded. A woman to whom Christ had said in startling intimacy, "We are one in love." A woman who had let God's words, "All shall be well," draw her courageously toward a realization of her visions in this unexpected form. She felt the presence of a person who had looked deep into the mystery of God and seen that in God there is no wrath, only love.

After a time—the convent quiet with its afternoon prayer and study—she returned to her desk. Dipping her quill in ink, straightening her shoulders, and drawing her breath into calm, she wrote:

> Here end the sublime and wonderful revelations
> of the unutterable love of God in Jesus Christ
> vouchsafed to a dear lover of his and in her to all
> his dear friends and lovers whose hearts, like hers,
> do flame in the love of our dearest Jesu.

Decade by decade, century by century, those who would be Christ's "dear friends and lovers" have turned to Julian, recognizing in her a sister and a friend, a fellow traveler. The book still seems to travel as it did from her window: hand to hand. The book contains a hidden story of a life rooted in a mysterious relationship of delight, a life staked in love and transformed by suffering. A life that blossoms forward to meet us, lit up by God's "endless kindness."

Acknowledgments

Lil Copan dreamed an idea with me at a pub in San Diego and went on to be a faithful steward of every word.

My guides in Norwich included the formidable Vivienne Bolton, who welcomed the stranger and told her about Key lime pie.

Sister Pamela at The Community of All Hallows, who among many other talents makes medlar and apple jam.

Tim Pestell at the Castle Archives.

Gudrun Warren at the Cathedral Library.

Carole Hill, a medieval historian with extraordinary insight into the life of fourteenth- and fifteenth-century Norwich. Her work provides much foundation for this story.

The librarians at the Lake County Library provided me a much-needed sanctuary, especially Nancy McCain, Janice Fox, Debbie Cisneros, and Shirley Crawford.

Bill Frank at the Colorado Mountain College library, who finds me many an obscure book, no questions asked.

Sarah Hankerson—researcher extraordinaire.

My father, Tom Johnson, for his library collection, wide-ranging knowledge, and willingness to take phone calls on any subject.

Mara Naselli, Kirsten Sampera, Ali Lufkin, Susan Fishman, Kira Cunningham, Lisa Morton, and Liz DaSilva, each of whom talked me through many a beginning and ending.

The Louisville Foundation for a Summer Stipend grant to research in Norwich.

Stephanie Frykholm—midwife of narrative.

Samuel Frykholm, because of whom I understood every word of Julian's writing better.

Peter, Joel, and Sam, who traveled far for this project.

Selected Bibliography

CONTEMPORARY VERSIONS OF JULIAN OF NORWICH'S WRITING:

Colledge, Edmund, and James Walsh, eds. *A Book of Showings to the Anchoress Julian of Norwich*, vols. 1–2. Toronto: Pontifical Institute of Medieval Studies, 1978.

Doyle, Brendan. *Meditations with Julian of Norwich*. Santa Fe: Bear and Company, 1983.

John-Julian, OJN, trans. *The Complete Julian of Norwich*. Brewster, MA: Paraclete Press, 2009.

Roden, Frederick. *Love's Trinity: A Companion to Julian of Norwich*. Translated by John-Julian, OJN. Collegeville, MN.: Liturgical Press, 2009.

Watson, Nicholas, and Jacqueline Jenkins, eds. *The Writings of Julian of Norwich: A Vision Showed to a Devout Woman* and *A Revelation of Divine Love*. University Park, PA.: Pennsylvania State University Press, 2006.

A SELECTION OF SECONDARY SOURCES:

Abbott, Christopher. *Julian of Norwich: Autobiography and Theology.* Rochester, NY: D.S. Brewer, 1999.

Aers, David, and Lynn Staley. *The Powers of the Holy: Religion, Politics and Gender in Late Medieval English Culture.* University Park, PA: Pennsylvania State University Press, 1996.

Atkinson, Clarissa. *The Oldest Vocation: Christian Motherhood in the Middle Ages.* Ithaca, NY: Cornell University Press, 1991.

Baker, Denise. *Julian of Norwich's Showings: From Vision to Book.* Princeton, NJ: Princeton University Press, 1994.

Bartlett, Ann Clark, Thoman Bestul, Janet Goebel, and William F. Pollard, eds. *Vox Mystica: Essays for Valerie M. Lagorio.* Rochester, NY: D.S. Brewer, 1995.

Bauerschmidt, Frederick Christian. *Julian of Norwich and the Mystical Body Politic of Christ.* South Bend, IN: University of Notre Dame Press, 1999.

Clark, Linda, ed. *The Fifteenth Century.* Rochester, NY: Boydell Press, 2006.

Clay, Rotha Mary. *The Hermits and Anchorites of England.* London: Methuen and Co., 1914.

Coakley, John. *Women, Men and Spiritual Power: Female Saints and their Male Collaborators.* New York: Columbia University Press, 2006.

Duffy, Eamon. *Marking the Hours: English People and Their Prayer Books.* New Haven, CT: Yale University Press, 2006.

————. *The Stripping of the Altars: Traditional Religion in England 1400–1580*. New Haven, CT: Yale University Press, 2005.

Gasquet, Francis Aidan. *Parish Life in Medieval England*. London: Methuen, 1922 (1906).

Gilchrist, Roberta, and Marilyn Oliva. *Religious Women in Medieval East Anglia: History and Archaeology: c.1100–1540*. Norwich, UK: Centre for East Anglian Studies, 1993.

Green, A.S. *Town Life in the Fifteenth Century*. New York: Macmillan, 1894.

Hale, Richard. *The Churches of King Street, Norwich in Medieval and Victorian Times*. Norwich, UK: King Street Publications, 1999.

Harper-Bill, Christopher, ed. *Medieval East Anglia*. Rochester, NY: Boydell Press, 2005.

Hill, Carole. "Incarnational Piety: Women and Religion in Late Medieval Norwich and its Hinterlands." Ph.D. diss., University of East Anglia, 2004.

————. "Julian and Her Sisters: Female Piety in Late Medieval Norwich," in *The Fifteenth Century*. Edited by Linda Clark. Rochester, NY: Boydell Press, 2006.

————. *Women and Religion in Late Medieval Norwich*. Rochester, NY: Boydell Press, 2009.

Jantzen, Grace. *Julian of Norwich: Mystic and Theologian*. New York: Paulist Press, 1988.

Jewson, Charles B. *People of Medieval Norwich*. Norwich, UK:

Jarrold and Sons, [ca. 1964].

Jones, E. A. *The Medieval Mystical Tradition in England: Exeter Symposium VII*. Rochester, NY: D.S. Brewer, 2004.

Kempe, Margery. *The Book of Margery Kempe*. Edited by Barry Windeatt. New York: Penguin Books, 1994.

Krantz, M. Diane F. *The Life and Text of Julian of Norwich: The Poetics of Enclosure*. New York: Peter Lang, 1997.

Leech, Kenneth, and Sr. Benedicta Ward. *Julian Reconsidered*. Fairacres, Oxford, UK: S.L.G. Press, 1988.

McAvoy, Liz Herbert, ed. *Companion to Julian of Norwich*. Rochester, NY: D.S. Brewer, 2008.

McEntire, Sandra J., ed. *Julian of Norwich: A Book of Essays*. New York: Garland Publishing, 1998.

Obbard, Elizabeth Ruth. *Introducing Julian Woman of Norwich*. London: New City, 1995.

———. *Through Julian's Windows: Growing into Wholeness with Julian of Norwich*. Norwich, UK: Canterbury Press, 2008.

Oliva, Marilyn. *The Convent and the Community in Late Medieval England: Female Monasteries in the Diocese of Norwich, 1350–1540*. Rochester, NY: Boydell Press, 1998.

Rawcliffe, Carol, and Richard Wilson, eds. *Medieval Norwich*. London and New York: Hambledon and London, 2004.

Renevey, Denis, and Christiania Whitehead, eds. *Writing Religious*

Women: Female Spiritual and Textual Practices in Late Medieval England. Toronto: University of Toronto Press, 2000.

Riddy, Felicity. "'Publication' before Print: The Case of Julian of Norwich," in *The Uses of Script and Print, 1300–1700.* Edited by Julian Crick and Alexandra Walsham. Cambridge, UK: Cambridge University Press, 2004.

Tanner, Norman. *The Church in Late Medieval Norwich, 1370–1532.* Toronto: Pontifical Institute of Mediaeval Studies, 1984.

Tuchman, Barbara. *A Distant Mirror: The Calamitous 14th Century.* New York: Knopf, 1978.

———. *Practicing History.* New York: Knopf, 1981.

Upjohn, Sheila. *In Search of Julian.* London: Darton, Longman and Todd, 1989.

———. *Why Julian Now: A Voyage of Discovery.* London: Darton, Longman and Todd, 1997.

Vinje, Patricia Mary. *An Understanding of Love According to the Anchoress Julian of Norwich.* Salzburg: Institut fur Anglistik und Amerikanistik, Universität Salzburg, 1983.

Wallace, May. *Medieval People of Norwich: Artists and Artisans.* Norwich, UK: King Street Publications, 1992.

Warren, Ann K. *Anchorites and Their Patrons in Medieval England.* Berkeley: University of California Press, 1985.

Notes

INTRODUCTION

ix   *English was rarely used*   Julian is a contemporary of
Geoffrey Chaucer, who was among the first to use
English to create literature.

x   *"The soul must perform two duties"*   *A Revelation of Love,* chapter
47. The translations from Julian's Middle English are, for
the most part, my own. I have used Nicholas Watson
and Jacqueline Jenkins's wonderful edition of Julian's
works, *The Writings of Julian of Norwich* (University Park, PA:
Pennsylvania State University Press, 2006). I have also
drawn a great deal of help and inspiration from Father John-
Julian's translation in *The Complete Julian of Norwich* (Brewster,
MA: Paraclete Press, 2008) and *Love's Trinity* (Collegeville,
MN.: Liturgical Press, 2008).

x   *oned*   Julian uses this expression for "united," but the
warmth of her English-root *one* instead of the colder Latin
root of *unite* conveys some of the sense of who God was
to her. Oneness was neither an abstract state nor a state
reached necessarily by a mystical act, but an ordinary state
of being.

x   *"desired . . . a bodily sickness"*   *A Revelation,* chapter 2.

xii *"thus I am safe"* *A Vision Shown to a Devout Woman*, section 6.

xiii *"even Christians"* "Even Christians" is a common expression in Middle English that generally refers to one's neighbors. It is like saying "fellow Christians," but also like saying "people just like me" or "ordinary folks."

xv *The Short Text* Watson and Jenkins call *The Short Text A Vision Shown to a Devout Woman*. In the excerpts used in this biography, I follow them and call this text *A Vision*. The longer, later version is called *A Revelation of Love*.

xv *"There is an anchoress"* Amherst Addl MS 37790.

xvii *Carole Hill* Personal conversation, May 11, 2009.

xix *"unlettered creature"* *A Revelation*, chapter 2.

EPIGRAPH

3 *the 13th day of May* The manuscripts vary on which day the visions begin. The Sloane manuscripts say "viii" and the Paris manuscript says "xiii." The church settled on May 8 for its traditional celebration while scholars have more recently tended toward May 13. Because the Paris manuscript appears to be older, I am using its date here.

THE FIRST WINDOW

6 *"evil tales of him to another?"* Eamon Duffy offers this as an example of the kinds of conversations conducted between

priest and parishioner in *Stripping the Altars: Traditional Religion in England 1400–1580* (New Haven, CT: Yale University Press, 2005), 59. He draws it from medieval manuscript St. John's MS S 35.

7 *"common teaching of Holy Church"*   *A Vision*, section 6.

7 *corbels*   Corbels are the figures, often whimsical, sometimes biblical, that fourteenth- and fifteenth-century craftsmen affixed to the joints of church roofs and beams.

8 *"cruel and oppressive"*   *A Revelation*, chapter 45.

8 *"beyond the common use of prayer"*   *A Revelation*, chapter 2.

8 *"minde"*   *A Revelation*, chapter 2. Translators have translated *minde* as recollection or memory, but we also need to include mindfulness and feeling in our understanding of the word's meaning.

12 *"lowly and simple things"*   *A Revelation*, chapter 32.

13 *kirtle*   A kirtle is a tunic-like piece of clothing common in medieval attire.

15 *"delving and dyking"*   *A Revelation*, chapter 51.

16 *medlar and pippens*   Both are fruits common in medieval times. The pippen was a small precursor to the modern apple. Medlar is a fruit still cultivated in England that is excellent for jam making because of its high natural pectin content.

17 *shrift and housel*   Medieval terms for confession and communion at the time of death. Both were felt to offer protection in the afterlife.

18 *"freely without any effort"*   A Revelation, chapter 2.

18 *St. Cecilia*   The version of St. Cecilia's story common in the Middle Ages came from *The Golden Legend,* a collection of stories of saints written in the twelfth century.

THE SECOND WINDOW

21 *travail*   Travail is a word that Julian often uses in combination with two other words: *pain* and *service. Travail* is a common word for a mother in childbirth, for Christ on the cross, and perhaps for a woman laboring for the survival of others, and failing, and watching people she loved die. If we understand the losses Julian suffered as coming from her own most intimate relationships, we begin to have a window into her attention to the problem of suffering. We will no longer hear her words, "All will be well," without knowing that she paid dearly for that understanding and resisted it for good reason.

24 *the mother of at least one child*   This is the most difficult period of Julian's life for a biographer to negotiate. Some scholars firmly believe that the evidence points to Julian's having become, by this time, a nun at nearby Carrow Abbey. Carrow Abbey, the convent that housed the daughters of Norwich's aristocrats, had a few dozen nuns at this time;

Julian is not listed among them, though perhaps she was there and unrecorded. Many of Carrow Abbey's records have indeed been lost in fires and to time. Her writing never refers to religious vocation, convents, prioresses, or sisters. She writes simply to her "even Christians." This makes the evidence that Julian was a nun slight, but it is at least an argument to explain how a woman gained such a striking education. Few paths were open to women for any education beyond embroidery.

But for me, the bigger problem with the theory that Julian was a nun is that it does not illuminate the deeper question: why did suffering become the focal point of Julian's theology? The possibility that Julian married, had children, and lost them in this ill-timed plague gives us an answer, however tentative, for why her wounds became deep enough to propel her from ordinary to extraordinary, from a thoughtful but still conventional woman to one restless enough to flout traditions.

25 *"as it fell to me to do"*   *A Revelation*, chapter 64.

25 *"bloated heap of stinking mire"*   *A Revelation*, chapter 64.

27 *"pull them out"*   Quoted in Carol Rawcliffe, "Health and Safety at Work in Late Medieval East Anglia," Christopher Harper-Bill, ed., *Medieval East Anglia* (Rochester, NY: Boydell, 2005), 137.

28 *"Why was the beginning of sin not prevented?"* *A Revelation*, chapter 27.

THE THIRD WINDOW

29 *bored and restless* I draw my suggestion that Julian faced boredom and loss of purpose during this period from an odd moment at the end of her visions. While the devil is tormenting her, she has the thought, "Now you have plenty to do . . . would you keep yourself free from sin, this would be a worthy occupation" (*A Revelation*, chapter 69). This, perhaps, implies that she had been looking for and struggling to find a "worthy occupation."

30 *"love-yearning"* *A Revelation*, chapters 31 and 40.

30 *living with her mother* Julian's writing offers us no clues about how she came to be living in her mother's household or her mother in hers at the time of her illness. The difficulty of imagining this transition should remind us that Julian's life is an enigma. Julian never mentions a husband or children. The only member of her family she discusses is her mother, and then only briefly.

31 *pyx* A pyx was the little box that priests used to transport the Eucharist. It was usually carried by a cord around their necks.

31 *"to thy glory?"* *A Vision*, section 2.

32 *intermediary* Julian frequently expresses her desire for a faith without intermediaries. This seems to be one of the central desires that the visions fulfill. See *A Revelation*, chapter 4, for example.

33 *pellets* A Revelation, chapter 7. A pellet was a processed grain. John-Julian, OJN, explains, "Pellets were small round balls of the meal made from any cereal" (*The Complete Julian of Norwich*, 409).

33 *"alive and active"* A Revelation, chapter 7.

33 *"soak the bed"* A Revelation, chapter 12.

33 *"the Fiend is overcome"* A Revelation, chapter 13.

33 *"I would not have asked"* A Revelation, chapter 19.

33 *"Look up to heaven"* A Revelation, chapter 19.

34 *"Lo, how I love thee"* A Revelation, chapter 24.

THE FOURTH WINDOW

35 *"Benedicite Dominus"; "Today is my Doomsday"; she laughed merrily* A Vision, section 5; A Revelation, chapters 8 and 13, respectively. *Benedicite Dominus* is grammatically incoherent in this setting, but the exchange in which a parishioner says, *"Benedicite"* (bless me), and a priest answers briefly, *"Dominus (te benedicat)"* (meaning "God will bless you"), was something Julian probably heard frequently in church and adopted as an expression.

36 *"weight of the body"* A Revelation, chapter 17.

36 *"Christ's pain in me."* This scene is given in *A Vision*, section 10.

37 *"homely and familiar"*   By homely, Julian does not mean ugly. Julian uses this word for the familiar, the simple, the domestic and the lowly, for the things of home that we find comforting. In Julian's vocabulary, God is homely as well as courtly, of the home as well as of the court. See *A Revelation*, chapter 5, for example.

37 *"nearest, readiest, surest"*   *A Revelation*, chapter 60. While medieval mothers are glorified in figures like St. Anne, the mother of Mary, and St. Bridget, the mother who became a saint in Julian's generation, actual mothers, with all of their imperfections, rarely appear in art, writing, music, or any other form of expression. That makes this gesture of Julian's own mother's hand extraordinary.

39 *"How do you fare?"*   This scene is recounted in *A Revelation*, chapter 66.

42 *"not be overcome"*   *A Revelation*, chapter 68.

42 *"I saw thee not"*   *A Vision*, section 23.

42 *"secret touching"*   *A Revelation*, chapter 43.

42 *what had been shown to her?*   *A Revelation*, chapters 47 and 70.

THE FIFTH WINDOW

44 *misericords*   A misericord is a piece of furniture found in medieval churches. The word comes from the Latin for "mercy seat." A misericord was a bench that people could lean on in church if they were sick or tired or old.

The intricately carved masterpieces from Norwich Cathedral that date from this period are striking examples of fourteenth-century craftsmanship.

46 *"it helpeth Christian men"*   This quotation is attributed to Wycliffe. See *The Select English Works of John Wyclif*, ed. Thomas Arnold, vol. 3 (Oxford: Clarendon Press, 1871), 184.

46 *Bishop Despenser*   Despenser was known for ostentatious displays of ego. Once when visiting the northern city of Lynn, a city that had a long-established tradition of independence, he insisted on carrying the mayor's mace in a parade through the town. Warned by the mayor that the people of Lynn would consider this a provocation, Despenser called them "ribaldos" and ignored this advice. He was pelted by stones and driven back from the city. He had to call in help from the king to get access to the city's ports. See "Julian of Norwich and the Crisis of Authority" in David Aers and Lynn Staley, *The Powers of the Holy: Religion, Politics and Gender in Late Medieval English Culture* (University Park, PA: State University of Pennsylvania Press, 1996), 156.

47 *friars and friaries in Norwich*   Julian does not say that the man at her bedside when she awakened from her visions was, in fact, a friar. To describe the first priest, who held the cross, she uses the word *curate*. A curate was a person with a specific role within a parish church. But to describe this second man, she uses the word *religious*, a vague word

for just about anybody who follows a monastic way of life. A monk, a friar, a priest—all were "religious." Monks were attached to monasteries. Priests were assigned to specific parishes with specific duties. Friars had less well-established roles and locations. They followed religious orders and were under the jurisdiction of the local bishop, but they were not as bound in many ways as other forms of "religious." They lived in houses within the city. They engaged in trade, raised sheep and crops, and had libraries. They often had higher degrees from Oxford, Cambridge, or Paris. But frequently, they were found on the streets with the people. They preached on street corners and in churches. They engaged people as spiritual advisors and confessors. One of the benefits of the friary was that friars, unlike monks, had a greater degree of autonomy. For this reason, I conclude that the man with whom Julian begins her education was a friar.

48 *Austin friars*   The Austin friars, also called the Augustinian friars, were particularly learned and respected in Norwich. Their friary was prosperous, and the Augustinian friars worked hard to earn the respect of their neighbors. They maintained ports and ran a fair business. They raised sheep and sold wool. Their reputation persisted up to the Reformation, when Henry VIII dissolved the monasteries and friaries and chased all "religious" into secular life or to the continent. Francis Blomefield, collecting a history of Norwich two hundred years after the Reformation, wrote of the Austin friars, "These friars, to do them justice, were

always reckoned a society of learned men, good disputants and eloquent preachers and were truly industrious in propagating literature."

51 *"still live in it?"* Romans 6:1–2, derived from the Latin Vulgate translation.

52 *not seeking attention for himself* In Norwich, some of the men who developed relationships of help and support with women are named in the historical record. Richard Caister, Richard Fernys, and William Southfield all helped women with their spiritual lives. None of these men fits exactly the time or the profile of the man who was at Julian's bedside, but they do fit the essence. Men of religious vocation educated and helped women along their spiritual way. Every person who studies Julian's writings eventually comes up against this conundrum: here was a woman who appeared to have extensive knowledge of St. Paul, St. Augustine, and St. Jerome. She articulated a unique form of mysticism that was not derived from the more famous mystical figures of her day, and she showed no relationship to them. Still more strangely, she actually wrote down what she saw without ever indicating that she had help. How did she receive an education? How did she do this writing?

Julian fit into a window of time when a few men were eager to hear women's voices and were not terrified of the consequences. Before Julian's death, the Archbishop of Canterbury, Thomas Arundel, reacted to fears of heresy and prohibited women from acting as teachers in any form.

The pope, too, responded harshly after Bridget's death to female visionaries. But for a brief period of time, men reached out to women and listened to them. Typically, such men left their mark on women's work. They wrote prefaces telling the circumstances of how they came to hear a woman's story or they signed their own names to the writing. Julian's case is remarkable because there is no record of a scribe. If there was such a mentor in Julian's life, and to me he is the best way to explain Julian's mysterious education, then he was, like Julian herself, remarkably self-hiding. I have found John Coakley's work *Women, Men and Spiritual Power* (New York: Columbia University Press, 2006) especially helpful in contextualizing Julian's possible education in this way.

THE SIXTH WINDOW

53 *they did not end*   *A Revelation*, chapter 70.

53 *"doubtful dread"*   *A Vision*, section 25.

54 *medled lyf*   Julian's contemporary, Walter Hilton, wrote a book of spiritual direction with this title. There is no evidence that Julian was acquainted with this work.

55 *"words formed in her understanding"*   *A Revelation*, chapter 9.

55 *"All shall be well"*   *A Revelation*, chapter 27.

55 *"to Thy creatures?"*   *A Revelation*, chapter 29.

56 *"the Great Deed"*   *A Revelation*, chapter 32.

56 *"bodily sight"*   A *Revelation*, chapter 9.

56 *"possess"* . . . *"lack"*   A *Revelation*, chapter 10.

56 *"wasting of time"*   A *Revelation*, chapter 76.

57 *she had seen nothing*   A *Revelation*, chapter 33.

57 *"somewhat eased"*   Julian uses this phrase frequently, as in *A Revelation*, chapter 53.

57 *ceilinged room*   Derived from *A Revelation*, chapter 45.

58 *a "simple thing," an "ordinary thing"*   A *Revelation*, chapter 50.

58 *"see it in Thee?"*   A *Revelation*, chapter 50.

58 *"For love"*   A *Revelation*, chapter 86.

60 *William Ufford*   Interestingly, William Ufford was the husband of Isabel Ufford, who after the Earl's death became an anchoress and supported Julian of Norwich. Some scholars think that Isabel and Julian may have had a long association that goes beyond Isabel's gift to Julian at the time of Isabel's death.

61 *straithe*   A straithe is a pier or a wharf.

61 *Julian had seen an "example"*   A *Revelation*, chapter 51. *Example* is the word that Julian uses, but *illustration* or *parable* might make more sense in contemporary English.

61 *"great slade"*   A *Revelation*, chapter 51.

61 *"assessed as precious"*   A *Revelation*, chapter 42.

62 *"marvelous melodies of endless love"* A Revelation, chapter 14.

62 *"lowest part of our need"* A Revelation, chapter 6.

62 *"oned together in love"* A Revelation, chapter 78.

THE SEVENTH WINDOW

63 *"fair, delectable place"* A Revelation, chapter 24. *Delectable* might be translated "pleasing," "desirable," or "delightful."

66 *"Know it now"* A Revelation, chapter 70.

67 *"fully as I should wish"* A Revelation, chapter 9.

67 *"that it do the same for you"* A Vision, section 13. In the next version of her writing, Julian tries several more ways to "translate" Jesus' saying, "Lo, how I love thee."

68 *"Is not Jesus the teacher of all?"* A Vision, section 6.

68 for the *"simple"* A Revelation, chapter 9.

69 *"Jesu the teacher of all"* A Vision, section 6.

70 *"I keep thee full safely"* A Vision, section 17.

70 *"all my even Christians"* A Vision, section 6.

THE EIGHTH WINDOW

71 *one small circle* Nearly every book written in the Middle Ages was written for a small, specific group. Most of the mystical writings that we have, such as those of Richard Rolle,

Walter Hilton, and Richard de Lampole are addressed to individuals, often women. Julian does not tell us anything of those to whom she writes, preferring the broadest term possible, "even Christians." Even so, by envisioning a circle of support for Julian, we can begin to imagine how the arrangements were made for her enclosure and how she gained enough support to enter the anchorage, and we gain at least a hint of why Julian's book has the quality of intimacy that it does.

71 *works of mercy*   The medieval church taught that there were seven "corporal works of mercy" that should be performed by all Christians. These were feeding the hungry, clothing the naked, giving drink to the thirsty, visiting the sick, burying the dead, sheltering the homeless, and visiting those in prison. Historian Carole Hill points out in her doctoral thesis that in medieval society these works, while belonging to all Christians, were primarily the responsibility of women. See Carole Hill, "Incarnational Piety: Women and Religion in Late Medieval Norwich and its Hinterlands" (Ph.D. diss., University of East Anglia, 2004), 17.

72 *"ghostly sights"*   Julian uses this phrase frequently. *Ghostly* translates simply as "spiritual," but again, the Latin root of *spirit* resonates differently than the English *ghost*, and our contemporary understanding of spirituality—very particular to our own time and place—makes Julian's word worth preserving, if only to remind us that Julian's understanding of God and how God is apprehended is different from our own.

72 *pursue a religious vocation*   Laywomen could follow several paths to make their holy pursuits more central to their lives. They could become vowesses and dedicate themselves to a particular order, receiving help from the nuns of that order. They could become corrodians and go to live on the grounds of a convent. Perhaps the highest calling was to become an anchoress. An anchoress was a person who dedicated herself to a particular patch of ground attached to a church. She withdrew from ordinary life, but she helped the people of the parish by praying for them and offering guidance. They helped her by providing food and fuel and a place of shelter. Once enclosed in an anchorage, a woman was able to dedicate herself fully to prayer.

73 *St. Julian's*   No one knows exactly when the church of St. Julian's was established on this particular spot in the Conesford area of Norwich. Some think that the Anglo-Saxon architecture (especially the round tower) points to an eleventh century or earlier construction. Others say it was built later but incorporated more ancient elements. Also difficult to trace is the origin of the name. Some say that it was named for St. Julian the Hospitaller, the patron saint of ferrymen and innkeepers. Others say the church is dedicated to St. Julian, Bishop of Le Mans. One of the difficulties in determining who Julian of Norwich was is that many have assumed that she took her name from the parish where she was in residence. John-Julian, OJN, has argued that this is an unnecessary assumption (*The Complete Julian of Norwich*, 21). Julian was

a popular woman's name in the fourteenth century. He then concludes that the anchoress Julian of Norwich was in fact Julian Erpingham Phelip, wife of an aristocratic citizen of Norwich. But because the dates do not match well and Julian's writings do not hint at an aristocratic background, his argument is not convincing (*The Complete Julian of Norwich*, 27).

74 *"half-sisters"*   Another example of the "mixed life," half-sisters were women who served in hospitals and poor houses, often independent of religious orders.

75 *pilch*   A pilch is a blanket made from animal fur.

78 *time of trial*   *A Revelation*, chapter 35.

79 *Bishop Despenser*   We have no way of knowing if Bishop Despenser himself conducted this ceremony. The bishop's leet rolls suggest that he was in Norwich a great deal more often during this period of his life (the early 1390s) than he was during the rest of his career. Bishop Despenser's biographers suggest that he was a man who loved ceremony and used his vicar general more rarely for ceremonies than other bishops. This means that the bishop himself could have conducted the ceremony. On the other hand, he may have sent his vicar general to enclose Julian. See Richard Allington-Smith, *Henry Despenser: The Fighting Bishop* (Norfolk, UK: Larks Press, 2003), 139.

79 *rood screen*   A rood screen is the carved wooden screen in a medieval church that separates the chancel from the nave.

79 *thurible*   A thurible is a metal censer in which incense is burned.

THE NINTH WINDOW

84 *a different man was appointed*   This was a practice called "choppechurching," and Bishop Despenser looked on in amusement as young churchmen jockeyed for better positions in the church hierarchy (See Richard Allington-Smith. *Henry Despenser: The Fighting Bishop*, 28). St. Julian's, as an urban church, was not a bad assignment, but there were plenty of wealthier parishes for an ambitious young rector to seek, so for a time, St. Julian's acted as a way station.

86 *"it is made endlessly holy"*   A Revelation, chapter 53.

86 *furmity*   Furmity is a porridge.

87 *his eternal dwelling*   A Revelation, chapter 67.

87 *Every showing was full of secrets*   A Revelation, chapter 51.

88 *sharpest throes and the hardest pains*   A Revelation, chapter 60.

88 *"I would suffer more"*   A Revelation, chapter 22.

88 *"For there is despair"*   A Revelation, chapter 17.

88 *yet we never come out of God*   A Revelation, chapter 5.

89 *"lighteninges and touchinges"*   A Revelation, chapter 65.

90 *"oneing you to myself"*   *A Revelation,* chapter 28.

91 *"am able to tell"*   *A Revelation,* chapter 37.

91 *The bitterness of doubt*   *A Revelation,* chapter 74.

THE TENTH WINDOW

94 *"ghostly and more sweetly"*   *A Revelation,* chapter 9.

95 *She walked over*   The reconstruction of Julian's cell that exists at the present day St. Julian's church in Norwich is situated on the south side of the building, attached to the church itself. Most of the remaining anchorite's cells in England are made of stone and attached to churches. The Norwich Historic Churches Trust, however, believes that the flint "foundation" on which the reconstruction of Julian's cell is based is more likely a buttress than her cell. An eighteenth-century map of St. Julian's shows a detached structure in the churchyard, labeled "Anchorite's Cell." This suggests that Julian's cell was perhaps a detached structure as the map shows. This means that she would have had to participate in mass through the "leper's squint"—a small window into the church usually located near the front of the nave.

97 *"learn to love God better"*   *A Vision,* section 4, and *A Revelation,* chapter 3.

97 *"rest in soul and a quietness in conscience"*   *A Revelation,* chapter 40.

97 *"love and fear are brothers"*   *A Revelation,* chapter 74.

THE ELEVENTH WINDOW

Case of Julian of Norwich," Julian Crick and Alexandra Walsham, eds., *The Uses of Script and Print, 1300–1700* (Cambridge, UK: Cambridge University Press, 2004), 29–49. A copy of Julian's book is recorded to have been in the impressive library at Syon Abbey before it was destroyed by fire.

105 *Countess Isabel Ufford's death*   The bequest of twenty shillings to Julian helps us to see Julian in what historian Carole Hill calls a "sphere of influence." Emma was enclosed in Norwich at the Whitefriars sometime after 1419. She died after only a little more than a year there. I especially like Carole Hill's essay on the subject of Julian's influence: "Julian and Her Sisters: Female Piety in Late Medieval Norwich," Linda Clark, ed., *The Fifteenth Century* (Rochester, N.Y.: Boydell Press, 2006).

106 *"cleave to the one Goodness"*   A Revelation, chapter 83.

106 *"endless day"*   A Revelation, chapter 83.

107 *"love God better"*   A Vision, section 6.

108 *"chapter houses"*   Scholars suggest that Julian's work was kept alive specifically in three communities: the Benedictines, who were significant in Norwich at the time; the Bridgetines, an order of men and women founded in the early fifteenth century to honor the newly sainted Bridget; and the Carthusians, whose "chapter houses" contained collections of personal accounts of mystical and spiritual experience.

108   *the dissolution*   In 1536, the English Parliament passed a law that any monastery with an income of less than 200 pounds a year would be closed and its wealth assumed by the government, but that rule quickly expanded to include all monasteries, convents, and friaries. Thousands of religious houses were dissolved, and King Henry VIII collected their assets.

EPILOGUE

109   *The older of the two*   (Sloane) MS 2499.

111   *This manuscript is smaller*   (Sloane) MS 3705.

Notes on the Artwork

The medallions running throughout the text of this book are renderings based on the marvelous roof bosses of the cathedral of Norwich. Over a thousand stone carvings in all, they run the length of the cathedral nave, transepts, and cloister roofs. Depicting Bible stories from creation to the Book of Revelation, scenes from popular Mystery Plays, lives of the saints, as well as the unique creatures, half-human and half-beast, who inhabit medieval myth and folklore, these vignettes offer a wide variety of medieval stories.

GOD THE CREATOR

CREATION OF EVE

ANGEL

THE NATIVITY

CALLING THE DISCIPLES

DOUBTING THOMAS

RIDER OF THE APOCYLPSE

SWAN

EAGLE

About Paraclete Press

WHO WE ARE

As the publishing arm of the Community of Jesus, Paraclete Press presents a full expression of Christian belief and practice—from Catholic to Evangelical, from Protestant to Orthodox, reflecting the ecumenical charism of the Community and its dedication to sacred music, the fine arts, and the written word. We publish books, recordings, sheet music, and video/DVDs that nourish the vibrant life of the church and its people.

WHAT WE ARE DOING

Books

PARACLETE PRESS BOOKS show the richness and depth of what it means to be Christian. While Benedictine spirituality is at the heart of who we are and all that we do, our books reflect the Christian experience across many cultures, time periods, and houses of worship.

We have many series, including *Paraclete Essentials; Paraclete Fiction; Paraclete Poetry; Paraclete Giants;* and for children and adults, *All God's Creatures,* books about animals and faith; and *San Damiano Books,* focusing on Franciscan spirituality. Others include *Voices from the Monastery* (men and women monastics writing about living a spiritual life today), *Active Prayer,* and new for young readers: *The Pope's Cat.* We also specialize in gift books for children on the occasions of Baptism and First Communion, as well as other important times in a child's life, and books that bring creativity and liveliness to any adult spiritual life.

The Mount Tabor Books series focuses on the arts and literature as well as liturgical worship and spirituality; it was created in conjunction with the Mount Tabor Ecumenical Centre for Art and Spirituality in Barga, Italy.

Music

THE PARACLETE RECORDINGS label represents the internationally acclaimed choir *Gloriæ Dei Cantores,* the *Gloriæ Dei Cantores Schola,* and the other instrumental artists of the *Arts Empowering Life Foundation.*

Paraclete Press is the exclusive North American distributor for the Gregorian chant recordings from St. Peter's Abbey in Solesmes, France. Paraclete also carries all of the Solesmes chant publications for Mass and the Divine Office, as well as their academic research publications.

In addition, PARACLETE PRESS SHEET MUSIC publishes the work of today's finest composers of sacred choral music, annually reviewing over 1,000 works and releasing between 40 and 60 works for both choir and organ.

Video

Our video/DVDs offer spiritual help, healing, and biblical guidance for a broad range of life issues including grief and loss, marriage, forgiveness, facing death, understanding suicide, bullying, addictions, Alzheimer's, and Christian formation.

Learn more about us at our website:
www.paracletepress.com, or call us toll-free at 1-800-451-5006.

You may also be interested in . . .

GIVE LOVE AND RECEIVE THE KINGDOM
THE ESSENTIAL PEOPLE AND THEMES
OF ENGLISH SPIRITUALITY

Benedicta Ward, SLG

ISBN 978-1-64060-097-3 • $24.99, Hardcover

*From the greatest living expert on the history of English spirituality
comes the most expansive collection ever published of her work*

FROM THE SPIRITUALITY OF CUTHBERT, TO BEDE AND THE PSALTER, Anselm the monastic scholar, and the depths of Julian of Norwich, from twelfth-century hermits, through medieval pilgrimage, and by illuminating seventeenth-century preachers, this volume is Benedicta Ward's magnum opus. With a title drawn from the writings of St. Anselm—a beautiful summary of the Christian life—this book is designed to both inspire and educate.

Lightning Source UK Ltd.
Milton Keynes UK
UKHW012343140322
400044UK00003B/938